LOVE QUEST

Love Quest

www.noahbolinder.com

First Edition

ISBN: 978-0-9958291-3-8 eBook

ISBN: 978-0-9958291-2-1 paperback

Published by:

Viking House Publishing

Victoria, BC, Canada.

LOVE QUEST

NOAH BOLINDER

For Fiona

TABLE OF CONTENTS

What is love?

– Haddaway

INTRODUCTION

THE TIPPING POINT happened on March 12th 2014.

I was driving to the Red Barn Market, a small local grocery store four minutes away from my house. I had to pick up a few items for supper. It was nothing flashy; just an ordinary thing to do on an ordinary day. After arriving at the store and finding what I needed, I made my way to the checkout where a female cashier about my age began ringing through the items. I didn't catch her name, but I would discover that it was Fiona.

Then it happened. It was a realization that crashed down on me amidst the beeping of the grocery scanner.

This girl did not know.

For a moment I looked directly into her eyes, but her gaze was fixed on the groceries. Truth be told, I couldn't have cared less about those few cans of food. What I was really interested in was *her*.

Did she see it? Did she know? No.

And with that my heart began to break. A quiet whirlwind of frustration began to stir deep within me. Oh how her life and perspective would change if she knew the truth. Those longings and desires in her heart were there for a reason, a reason beyond her wildest dreams. If only I had the time and opportunity to share with her. But that seemed impossible. I knew what was about to happen. Within a few short seconds I would pull out my debit card, tap some numbers on a machine, say thank you, and leave. It was all very predictable. In less than a minute I was walking out of the store.

I laid the bag she had packed on the adjacent seat in my car and turned on the ignition. My hand gripped the steering wheel with extra firmness as I pulled out of the parking lot.

This girl had to know! Someone had to tell her. But who? Who was going to tell her?

Then it happened. In an instant, I knew.

I was the one who would tell her.

As I turned left onto the main road, I knew a fire had been lit in my soul. Yes, this *needed* to happen. This was *going* to happen. This story was too important to sit on. I would write a book: this book. I would write it for the girl at the checkout counter and the countless others who needed to encounter this story. It's the story that has changed and continues to change my life. I hope it will do the same for you as it has for me.

Noah Bolinder

ONE

THE MAIN EVENT

APRIL 5TH, 2002.

The arena is packed with thousands of basketball fans that have gathered from across the city to see the Philadelphia 76ers play the visiting Detroit Pistons. An eleven year old girl listens to the beating of music and rumbling of the crowd as she stands just out of sight down a hall near the stadium floor. Her heart pounds in sync with the music and she folds her hands, trying to appear calm.

"It's time," the attendant next to her says as he steps forward out of the hall towards the court and motions for her to follow.

Her heart skips a beat.

Within a matter of seconds she is in view of thousands of people. As she takes her position, the music suddenly fades.

She swallows.

The moment she was waiting for had arrived. "Now ladies and gentleman," the thundering voice of the announcer echoed through the building, "at this time we ask that you please rise and remove your caps for the singing of the national anthem, being performed tonight by…" Then she hears the words.

Her name.

A smile breaks across her face. All these people had heard *her* name. In a moment, following a brief pause, the announcer's voice was replaced by her own.

She was living her dream.

As the song ended, the crowd cheered and she raised her hand to wave. She had done it. The main event of the night was now over.

Yet for the crowd, the night was just beginning. The singing of the national anthem was a necessary ritual, but not what they had paid to see. The name of the girl who sang for them passed through their minds as soon as she had finished.

It was a close game, but the Pistons defeated the 76ers 92-88. Another loss. People began leaving and within an hour the arena was empty. The building so full of life a moment before was now eerily quiet.

What was so special about this game? Hundreds of NBA games take place every year. The match between the 76ers and the Pistons should have long since faded into history. But here it is, discussed in the opening chapter of this book. There is one small detail about this game on April 5th 2002 that has preserved its memory.

The girl.

While she sang, the crowd thought they were waiting for the main event, but they were wrong. Hidden in plain sight, they watched the main event pass them by. Leaving the arena that night, one person knew what had really happened. Maybe, she wondered, one day they would look back and see too.

* * *

March 18th, 2010.

The stadium is packed with thousands of fans that have come from across the state to see the show. A 19-year-old girl listens to the beating of music and the screams of the crowd as she stands hidden out of sight below the stage. Her heart pounds and she takes a deep breath to steady herself.

"It's time," the director says to her. "Thirty seconds." Her eyebrows jump with excitement as she looks back at her team with a final smile before hurrying into position.

Her heart skips a beat.

Within a matter of seconds she will be in view of thousands of people. The music begins to play and she feels the elevator lifting her to the stage. The screams of the crowd intensify.

She swallows.

Is it really possible? Eight years ago she sang here for a 76ers game. Now they had come to see her, the main event. It was the moment she was waiting for, and this time playing here was particularly special because tonight was the moment *they* were waiting for too. Her head emerges from the stage. As she continues to rise, the audience sees she is dressed in a white marching band uniform. She hears the crowd chanting…

Her name.

A smile breaks across her face. These people are calling *her* name. And now it was time to sing, but this time is was not the national anthem.

The song she begins to sing is *You Belong With Me*, and the girl is Taylor Swift. Tonight the crowd would not forget her name. Tonight their eyes were opened. She had never been the sideshow. She was the main event.

* * *

By her early twenties, Taylor Swift had taken the world by storm. She became the youngest person in history to win a Grammy for Album of the Year and the only female artist to have back-to-back albums sell over a million copies in the first week. *Time* magazine named her one of the top 100 influential people in the world and in 2011 *Billboard* selected her as Woman of the Year. She was able to sellout the massive Madison Square Garden arena in New York City in 60 seconds and her estimated net worth is over $200 million.[1] There is no denying Taylor's astounding success, but what is it about her brand that has turned her into an international sensation? There are many reasons: she is attractive, talented and writes her own music. But what brings these things together is the content of her songs. She writes about love and relationships: the ecstasy and tragedy. What's more, she writes about her personal experiences with love.

Humans are naturally drawn to love stories. Finding love and pursuing romance resides at the core of who we are. Turn on the radio and most of the songs are about relationships, the good, the bad and ugly. The top selling genre for books are romance novels on which people spend over a billion dollars each year.[2] Watch any movie or TV show and romance is bound to make up at least part of the plot. Even advertisements try to associate love and romance with products. It's no accident advertisers try to make this association.

They know we are obsessed.

The vast majority of people will get married at least once in their lifetime. We see marriage as a normal and natural thing people do, and it is, but it's also very radical. Just think about it. Marriage is the merging of all your possessions, all your money, your home and very life with another person. It involves forsaking all other potential lovers and living alongside a particular human being for the rest of your life. And why do most of us make this seemingly insane choice?

Love.

A small word most of us don't know how to define that drives our existence. What is it about the opposite sex that fascinates our hearts and draws us toward each other? In the 1970s many people began arguing that men and women were essentially the same and gender roles were almost entirely shaped by society. If culture could just lose its bias and treat boys and girls exactly the same, men and women would grow up without acting so different from each other. Gender distinguishes us on the outside, but inside we are pretty much the same.

Today, with the help of magnetic resonance imaging (MRI), we are able to look inside our brains and science has resoundingly debunked the idea that men and women are practically the same. Men and women's brains live in different worlds and function very differently.[3] There are many books that talk about the differences between male and female brains, but what about the differences in our hearts? If science is showing that men and women *are* in fact different, could it be that we also have different desires in our souls? Deep down, what are the central things we long for?

In the book *Wild at Heart: Discovering the Secret of a Man's Soul,* John Eldredge says there are three desires in the hearts of men.

- A battle to fight.
- An adventure to live, and
- A beauty to rescue.[4]

In the book *Captivating: Unveiling the Mystery of a Woman's Soul*, the sequel to *Wild at Heart*, John and Stasi Eldredge share what they believe are the three heart desires in women.

- To be romanced.
- To play an irreplaceable role in a great adventure, and
- To unveil beauty.[5]

While it may be challenging to enter a science lab and test if these statements are true, we can look to something else that should give us a clear idea whether or not the Eldredges are on the right track.

Hollywood.

Think of your typical action-adventure movie. There is a battle to fight, an adventure to live, and always a beauty to rescue. What about superhero films? Same thing. A good drama usually has a love interest, a woman who gets caught up in an adventure and captures a man's heart. How about romantic comedies? There's romance, adventure and conflict, and in the end the woman's beauty overcomes the man and they live happily ever after.

The number one selling entertainment line in the world is Disney Princess, a multibillion dollar industry. What is it about princesses that girls love? Princesses are always beautiful, pursued by handsome suitors and part of a grand adventure. But most importantly, princesses live happily ever after. Next to Disney Princess, the bestselling entertainment line is Star Wars.[6] I am one of the many boys that grew up loving Star Wars and was hooked the moment I started watching the films. The adventure and battle spans an entire galaxy and there's also usually a princess somewhere in the mix. Safe to say, I think the Eldredges are onto something. If all this about the longings in the hearts of men and women is true, we are confronted with an important question. *Where did these longings come from?*

The Hopeless Quest

There are two possible answers to this question. Either these longings were placed in us over millions of years through the process of natural selection or these longings were given to us by God. One story tells us that these longings evolved to prolong the species; the other says they were placed in us to reveal something about the heart of God.

We are faced with two stories. What are their implications? Let's take a moment to examine them. If the first story is true, if God does not exist, what is the destiny of Taylor Swift? What is the fate of the one who has achieved the very peak of success? How does her story end?

Unfortunately, this story is a tragedy.

Time will pass, and, slowly, inevitably, Taylor's natural beauty will fade. Her voice will grow weak and her songs will feel the strain of age. A point will come when her career will plateau and begin the process of decline. Each day, her songs will be played less and less and her name will be replaced by others. She will retire and her health will fail. Then she will die.

The end.

A hole will be dug in the ground and her body left in it to rot. The name Taylor Swift will continue to live on for a time in some circles, but eventually it will only be remembered by the odd music historian. Yes, in due time her own relatives will not even realize she existed.

But it gets worse. Scientists tell us that the entire universe will ultimately be destroyed in a heat death. No one will survive. There will come a point when Taylor Swift will literally be forgotten forever. Not a single soul will remember her, ever.

If the name and memory of Taylor Swift are destined to disappear, how much sooner will our names fade away? In this story called life, we all share the same tragic fate as Taylor Swift. We die, we rot, and our names are forgotten forever.

And how does love fair in this story? What do we discover is the true meaning of love? In a story where earth and humanity arise through a freak act of nature all on its own, love becomes a tool. Love is nothing but a set of chemical reactions that evolved to trick your brain into having sex with people for the survival of the species. That's it.

There is nothing special about falling in love. There is no difference between falling in love and your stomach digesting food. It's just a biological reaction. How sad it is to realize the joke is on us. If the meaning of love is to create more humans, we are trapped in a hopeless quest because we already know the end of the story. Humanity dies. No matter how strong of a species we create, we cannot avoid our date with destiny. To think of all the songs, all the books, all the movies that have depicted the supremacy of love, while all along it has been a pathetic, lingering illusion.

If love is a mirage and life disappears into nothingness,

what are we to live for? If we share the same fate as Taylor Swift, perhaps the best we can hope for is to achieve a taste of her success. If we set our mind to the pursuit of money, fame, beauty, or even the illusion of love, the things culture preaches will satisfy our hearts, then maybe we can at least savor the fleeting joys of life and forget the distasteful reality that one day it will all come crashing down.

What are the odds you will reach Taylor's status in fame, wealth or beauty?

Not good.

Even if you devoted your life to chasing any one of these things and you somehow made it, would your success be worth it? In the end, does reaching the top satisfy the heart? I wonder if Taylor gives us an answer in her song *The Lucky One* which is about a celebrity who makes it big but decides to run away from it all.

We have bought into the lie that *if I can just get that thing, then I'll be happy.* We hear the people at the top telling us this is not the case, but we ignore them. We won't believe it until we experience it ourselves.

With her success, wealth, beauty and fame, one would think finding true love for Taylor would be a blissful and easy task. She has dated many famous bachelors and countless men would do anything to win an outing with her. Yet mixed within her songs detailing the thrills of love are stories of heartache and betrayal. In her album cover for *Red* she writes,

> [T]here's something to be learned from waiting all day for a train that's never coming. And there's something to be proud of about moving on and realizing

> that real love shines golden like starlight, and doesn't fade or spontaneously combust. Maybe I'll write a whole album about that kind of love if I ever find it. But this album is about the other kinds of love that I've recently fallen in and out of. Love that was treacherous, sad, beautiful, and tragic.[7]

There is a sense of wonder but also a great heaviness in the kinds of love she describes. There's even an air of uncertainty in her words about whether or not she'll ever discover *real love*. In an interview with *The Guardian*, Taylor said, "I think the one thing I'm really afraid of is that the magic doesn't last. The butterflies and daydreams and love, all these things I hold so dear, are going to leave some day. I haven't had a relationship that's lasted forever."[8] Why is it that we desire a relationship where the magic never fades; for one that lasts forever? Is this longing based on fantasy, or does it point us to something more?

So far we have been talking about life and love in light of the first story: the story of the universe without God. If this story is true, Taylor's fear of losing it all is very real. There is nothing magical or eternal about love. It is a chemical reaction. The story of mankind and the story of love are the ultimate tragedy because in the end no one remembers us, everyone dies and there is no hope for a new beginning.

But what if I told you there was a different story? A story about love and life beyond your wildest dreams. A story in which you do not play an insignificant role destined to be forgotten, but a leading role at the very heart of the adventure.

The Grail Quest

One day as a child my family took me to a forest outside Vancouver. I had never been there before and on the drive over they told me a story about a great lost treasure that was still hidden in the park. While walking along the trail we came across a small bottle that contained a treasure map. We followed the directions that eventually led us off the trail where we found a large "X" marked by two fallen branches. There we began to dig. To my astonishment we found a treasure chest that was filled with jewelry and gold. As we walked back to the car I was jumping with excitement and exclaimed to people passing by that we had found the lost treasure. Several months later I inquired why we hadn't been on the news for finding the treasure and my parents told me it wasn't real. It had been a setup planned by my aunt for my entertainment.

Stories of lost treasure have always fascinated me. I remember lying in bed as a young boy and listening to my dad tell tales of lost gold mines across the world. Perhaps the ultimate treasure that has been pursued by generations is the Holy Grail. The legend of the Grail as the cup that Jesus drank from at the Last Supper can be traced back to the French poet Robert de Boron's work Joseph of Arimathea which was written around 1200AD. One of my favourite movies growing up was *Indiana Jones and the Last Crusade* where the Grail is shown to have the power to heal fatal gunshot wounds and provide eternal life. Despite hundreds of years passing, modern culture continues to be stirred by the mystery and pursuit of the Grail.

Recently two Spanish historians claimed to have located the Grail inside a Basilica in northern Spain which attracted a considerable amount of media attention. Commenting on the discovery, a writer in the *Independent* said bluntly, "It is, of course, a load of rubbish."[9] On the Grail, medieval historian Richard Barber states, "You can't find it and you won't find it. It is the ultimate unattainable object, a mystery that, because you cannot solve it, only becomes more attractive."[10]

In 2013 a couple in California were walking their dog along a trail on their property which they had gone down almost every day for years, but this time they spotted something. The side of a small rusted can was protruding out of the ground. They picked up a stick and used it to dig around the can which was sealed on both sides. Picking it up, they began making their way home. It was unusually heavy and they had to stop for a breather. Back home they opened it and were astonished to discover it was full of $20 American gold coins from the 1800s. They returned to the site the next day and went on to find five more cans full of gold. For years the couple had been walking past over 1,400 gold coins worth millions of dollars.[11]

Countless times the couple had walked by this great treasure. Similarly, what if we have walked by and missed the real treasure of the Grail. It is easy to dismiss the Grail as a fantasy because most of the stories surrounding it are fictitious. But did the Grail actually exist? If you are speaking of the cup that Jesus drank from at the Last Supper, then certainly. The truth is that the Grail does not contain magical powers, as depicted in *Indiana Jones*. But what if the real mystery and wealth of the Grail is found not in the physical cup itself, but in what it represents.

On the night of the Last Supper, the Gospel of Luke records that Jesus took a cup of wine and announced that it was "the new covenant in my blood".[12] Jesus was speaking to his *Jewish* disciples who would have been immersed in *Jewish* culture and intimately knew the *Jewish* scriptures. The vast majority of us today are oblivious to ancient Jewish culture and scriptures which is why the secret of the Grail has largely remained hidden. Our journey through this book will seek to unlock the mystery.

When Jesus took the cup at the Last Supper, he was making a statement on the meaning of love, marriage, gender and life itself. When Jesus took the cup at the Last Supper, he was revealing to us a different story.

This book is about that story.

Love Quest

To understand the meaning and significance behind the historical Grail we must embark upon a journey.

The Merriam Webster Dictionary defines *quest* as:

- *A journey made in search of something.*
- *A long and difficult effort to find or do something.*
- *A chivalrous enterprise in medieval romance usually involving an adventurous journey.*[13]

This book is about a quest to find the true meaning and story of love revealed in the Grail. The mystery we face is similar to a puzzle. Puzzles take time and effort to complete, especially if they are complex. Starting the puzzle is always most challenging, but as one slowly works to connect the pieces, a picture begins to take shape. Do not be fooled by what first appears as blotches of random colour. As our journey progresses, you will see these seemingly insignificant pieces form an intricate canvas.

Our quest will be one of adventure, romance and mystery. We seek to glance into the meaning of some of the world's most sacred things: love, marriage, gender and life itself. Some may consider these huge topics impossible to unlock, and they may be right. But then again, maybe they're wrong.

Like any good mystery, there will be clues. At the end of each chapter you will find a summary section where important details will be listed. You may not know what to do with these puzzle pieces immediately, but over time you will begin making connections.

Our quest to discover the mystery of the Grail begins with an examination of the ancient Jewish scriptures which Jesus' disciples would have known and studied. These texts have been translated into hundreds of languages and are a part of the bestselling book of all time with billions of copies in circulation.[14]

The Bible is one of the most loved and controversial books ever written. Many people argue that the Bible is the divinely inspired word of God. Others believe it is nothing more than a series of ancient legends and inspiring literature. You may not believe the Bible is God's word, yet Jesus and his disciples did. To fully understand the mystery of the Grail that Jesus communicated to his disciples at the Last Supper, we must enter into the story of these ancient Jewish texts and attempt to understand them. Only then will we be able to unlock the true mystery behind the most sought after relic of all-time.

Let the quest begin.

Key Points:

- Men desire a battle to fight, an adventure to live, and a beauty to rescue. Women desire to be romanced, to play an irreplaceable role in a great adventure, and unveil beauty.
- Money, fame and beauty do not ultimately satisfy the human soul.
- During the Last Supper Jesus used the Grail to unveil the meaning of love, marriage, gender and life.
- To unlock the mystery of the Grail, we must enter the story of the Jewish scriptures.

TWO

BEFORE THE BEGINNING

In the beginning God created the heavens and the earth.

- Genesis 1:1

THE BIBLE OPENS in the book of Genesis with God creating the world. When God makes man in the first chapter of the Bible, the story of humanity begins. But *our story* is not the beginning of *the story*. According to the Jewish scriptures, God has eternally existed outside of time and the physical universe.[15] It is within God's story that our story was birthed.

When working on a large puzzle it is a good strategy to find the corner pieces so you can begin to form the border. Once you have established the outline, there is a frame to work with and you can focus on piecing together the center of the image. Before diving into *our story*, it will be helpful to peer into the greater story from which we came.

The first important question to ask is, who is God? The picture the Bible gives us of God is a great mystery as it speaks of him as Father, Son and Holy Spirit. One God in essence, three in person. This idea of God's nature is known as the Trinity. There is nothing in the universe that compares with the Trinity, which makes it an extremely challenging concept to demonstrate and comprehend. The Bible is clear that there is only one eternal God and yet he has three distinct personal expressions. *Why is God like this?* It seems awfully confusing and unnecessary. Why isn't he just one simple being with one expression of himself? Wouldn't that be much easier for our minds to understand?

It *would* be easier for us to understand in our limited three-dimensional bodies, but if God only had a single personal expression he could not have always been a God of love. Let's unpack this. Love is something you have for another.

What do we call people who will do anything to benefit themselves?

Narcissists.

What do we call people who will do anything to benefit another?

Heroes, or, in many cases, lovers.

Love involves sacrificing oneself for the benefit of *another*. A God with a single personal expression could not be a God of love until he created someone *to* love. This God could have been all-powerful and all-knowing before he created anything, but he could not have had love at the core of his being. But the Bible is very clear when it tells us that God *is* love.[16] The triune nature of God explains to us how God has love in his essence because the members of the Trinity have eternally been in loving relationship with one another. Without relationship, true love is impossible.[17] What is immediately confusing about the Trinity is that we are dealing with one God but three persons who possess the identical divine nature. One key difference between the Father, Son and Spirit is their roles within the relationship. The Father stands in the highest position of authority in the Trinity.[18] He is the one to which all glory and honour is ultimately directed by the Son and Spirit. But the Father does not hoard this glory for himself, he reflects it back on the Son. The life of the Trinity forms a kind of dance where each person redirects glory and honour towards another. Novelist and Oxford scholar C.S. Lewis writes, "…God is not a static thing…but a dynamic, pulsating activity, a life, almost a kind of drama. Almost, if you will not think me irreverent, a kind of dance."[19] What are some clues about God we discover once we begin to see the life of the Trinity? While each member of the Trinity is fully God, each has a distinct role. The Son and Spirit live to glorify the Father and choose to submit to his direction, yet the Father does not hoard the glory reflected upon him for himself. This reveals God's giving nature. It is within this loving relationship that God has always experienced perfect happiness. Tim Keller expresses this point when he writes,

> "Imagine there is someone you admire more than anyone else in the world. You would do anything for him or her. Now imagine you discover that this person feels exactly the same about you, and you enter into either a lifelong friendship or a romantic relationship and marriage. Sound like heaven? Yes,

because it comes from heaven – that is what God had known within himself but in depths and degrees that are infinite and unimaginable. That is why God is infinitely happy, because there is an 'other-orientation' at the heart of his being, because he does not seek his own glory but the glory of others."[20]

The First Love Song

Now that we have briefly glimpsed into the life and nature of the one who created the universe, let's return to Genesis 1:1. *In the beginning God created the heavens and the earth.*[21] The word for "God" used in the original Hebrew is *Elohim*, a plural noun which echoes God's Trinitarian nature. In the first chapter of the Bible, God creates the sun, moon, stars, plants and animals. Then on the sixth day of creation he does something out of the ordinary. He designs something in his *own* image.

> *"Then God said, "Let us make human beings in our image, to be like us. They will reign over the fish in the sea, the birds in the sky, the livestock, all the wild animals on the earth, and the small animals that scurry along the ground."* ***27*** *So God created human beings in his own image. In the image of God he created them; male and female he created them."*
>
> (Genesis 1:26-27)

The triune God created man in *his* image. This is

fascinating. How is humanity created to be like the Trinity? If we read Genesis 2 carefully, we may find answers.

In Genesis 2:7-8 we see God create Adam and place him in a garden called Eden which means "delight".[22] But God sees a problem. Adam is alone.

> *"Then the LORD God said, "It is not good for the man to be alone. I will make a helper who is just right for him."...**21** So the LORD God caused the man to fall into a deep sleep. While the man slept, the LORD God took out one of the man's ribs and closed up the opening. **22** Then the LORD God made a woman from the rib, and he brought her to the man."*
>
> (Genesis 2:18, 21-22)

We learn that the "helper" God creates for man is the woman who is called Eve. To us, the word *helper* may sound second-class or even offensive, like God was creating a secretary for Adam, but this is not the case. The word *helper* is "*ezer*" which can be translated as "partner".[23] In fact, "ezer" is a word used to describe God in the scriptures.

> *"We put our hope in the LORD. He is our help [ezer] and our shield."*
>
> (Psalm 33:20)[24]

God forms the woman from one of Adam's ribs, and the Hebrew word translated "ribs" is the same word translated "side".[25] The woman comes from Adam's side, the middle of the man. She is neither above nor below him. She is his equal.

What is also interesting is the phrase used in Genesis 2:22 to describe God presenting her to Adam, "*...and he brought her to the man.*" The Hebrew used here is the same language a Jewish father used when presenting his daughter to the groom at a wedding.[26] Upon seeing the woman, Adam can barely contain himself.

> *""At last!" the man exclaimed. "This one is bone from my bone, and flesh from my flesh! She will be called 'woman,' because she was taken from 'man." **24** This explains why a man leaves his father and mother and is joined to his wife, and the two are united into one."*
>
> (Genesis 2:23-24)

On these verses John Mark Comer writes,

> "Notice that the first words out of a human's mouth in the Scriptures are a love song. And with a smile on his face, God joins in the song and says, "That is why a man leaves his father and mother and is united to his wife, and they become one flesh." When God said that, God created marriage. Did you catch that? God created marriage. This whole thing was his idea."[27]

Marriage is not something designed by man; marriage is designed by God. So here we are, witnessing the first marriage between a man and a woman in a garden called "delight."

Okay. Why?

Why did God create man, woman and the institution of marriage? What is his reason for starting this story? To understand, we must return to the Trinity. Some have suggested that God created humans to worship him because he wanted a self-esteem boost, but this certainly could not be the case because God has always been perfectly satisfied in his Trinitarian relationship. This also refutes the idea that God created mankind because he was lonely. What then would compel God to create us? Perhaps some light can be shed on this question by asking another.

Why do we create humans? What is the purest and healthiest reason for a couple to have a child? Greg Brezina writes,

> "As a healthy couple is to birthing babies, so is God to creating humanity. It is an unhealthy couple who says, "Let's have babies so we will have someone to love us." "Let's have children so they will serve us." "Let's have children so we can boss them around." "Let's have children so we can get praise from their success." On the other hand, it is the healthy couple who says, "Because we have an abundance of love in our marriage, let's share it. Let's have babies who will look like us, have our life within them, and love like us. Then they can enjoy an intimate love relationship with us." It is this couple's pure love that motivates them to give children life. In eternity, I imagine God having a holy huddle and saying, "We have such a great life together and an overabundance of love, let's share it. Let us make humanity in our image so that they can love like us. Then they can enjoy an intimate relationship with us."[28]

At the very heart of God is perfect self-giving love. This is the reason he began our story. He didn't need us to satisfy himself in anyway. God simply desired to share with us the amazing gift of himself. And where does God point to give us a picture of this divine love?

Marriage.

Genesis 2:24 says, "*This explains why a man leaves his father and mother and is joined to his wife, and the two are united into one.*" The word "one" translated from Hebrew is "echad" which is the same word used to describe the oneness of God. In the book of Deuteronomy it says, "*Hear, O Israel: The LORD our God, the LORD is one [echad].*"[29] The Bible teaches that when a man and woman are joined in marriage they become one, just as the Trinity is one. This means that within marriage, sex points us to the joy and intimacy of God's union. This is why God designed sex to be one of the most intense and physically satisfying experiences.[30] This also means that sexuality is *sacred* because it was created *by* God to reveal him.

God created sex and marriage to go together. Just as God took great delight in creating mankind in *his* image, so too has he designed us to take delight in the act of becoming one and creating children in *our* image. The first command given to mankind in Genesis 1:28 is, "*Be fruitful and multiply.*" In other words, *have sex*! The pleasure God has given us through sex is meant to reflect a tiny fraction of the joy he shares in the Trinity, and the delight we have as parents for our children provides a glimpse of God's fatherly love for us.

God designed marriage to give us a picture of himself: a permanent relationship of persons coming together in oneness who are fully committed to living for the love of the other. If this is true, then marriage is not about you. Marriage is about serving your spouse because marriage is a sacred institution designed to glorify and reflect God.

The secret for a thriving marriage is found in the Trinity. If the trinity is a dance, marriage is a dance, and the secret to the dance is giving glory to the other through selfless love. If you allow your movements around the other to become about glorifying and satisfying yourself, you will ultimately destroy the beauty of the dance. However, when both partners allow the dance to focus on the other, they are granted a small taste of the inner life of God.

Why is it that most people choose to unite their life with someone in marriage? Could it be that the God of true love has designed marriage as the closest human expression of the glorious relationship he has within himself? If so, and we are created to desire his perfect love, it makes sense that humanity has thrown itself at the feet of romance, desperately seeking what it is designed for: relationship with God. Only God can satisfy the soul's ache for love because the best human marriage is only a shadow of the love God shares in himself.

Returning to the story, in Genesis 1:26 God says, "*Let us make human beings in our image, to be like us.*" The following verse goes on to say, "*So God created human beings in his own image. In the image of God he created them; male and female he created them.*" God creates two kinds of humans: male and female.

So why did God create gender in humanity? This is a topic that will be touched on in the future, but perhaps we can discover some clues from the information we have already encountered. Since we know that humanity is created in the image of a triune God, let's look to compare gender with the Trinity and see if we discover any similarities.

First, God says both genders are created in *his* image. From this we can conclude that both genders are fully equal in value because *both* display God's image.[31] Likewise, the members of the Trinity are fully equal. The Bible also teaches that within marriage, the husband is to lovingly and sacrificially lead his family. This too is in line with the Trinity because each member of the Godhead is fully equal yet there is also an authority structure. In Western culture we tend to think of anyone in a place of authority as superior to a person in submission, but the Trinity defies this cultural perception. The Trinity is completely equal and yet God joyfully serves in positions of authority *and* submission. Submission is not something negative or second-rate. Submission is divine.

These clues hint that God reveals himself through both genders. By seeking to understand our own gender, the opposite sex, and God's plan for marriage, we just might be able to gain a deeper understanding of God's plan for humanity.

Breaking the Dance

The final verse of Genesis 2 ends with a surprising detail.

> *"Now the man and his wife were both naked, but they felt no shame."*
>
> (Genesis 2:25)

Why has it probably never seriously crossed your mind to walk downtown naked? First, stripping down in public might be illegal and second, it would be humiliating. But *why* would it be humiliating? When our nakedness is bared for all to see there is a deep sense of shame. This is not true with animals. It is a distinctly human experience.

Shame is not a positive emotion. People do not wake

up thinking about how they can experience shame. If God's original plan was for humans to be naked without shame, clearly something went wrong.

In Eden, Adam and Eve lived as God lives, with perfect love towards one another. Selfishness did not exist to poison relationships and cause shame. Christopher West writes,

> "We cover our bodies in a fallen world because they are so good and we feel an instinctive need to protect the goodness of the body from the degradation of lust. In the beginning, before sin, man and woman did not experience shame precisely because they did not experience lust. This does not mean they did not experience sexual desire. Rather, it means their erotic desire was not tainted by selfishness."[32]

Lust's focus is on pleasing itself. It is a perversion of the true love of God which is self-giving. There was no shame in nakedness in the garden because Adam and Eve were sinless and neither of them was focused on taking advantage of the other's body. Their natural disposition was to serve each other.

Today we are no longer living in this garden paradise, so what happened? We learn in Genesis 2 that God created one tree that was off limits to Adam and Eve.

> *"Then the Lord God planted a garden in Eden in the east, and there he placed the man he had made.* ***9*** *The Lord God made all sorts of trees grow up from the ground—trees that were beautiful and that produced delicious fruit. In the middle of the garden he placed*

> *the tree of life and the tree of the knowledge of good and evil...* ***15*** *The LORD God placed the man in the Garden of Eden to tend and watch over it.* ***16*** *But the LORD God warned him, "You may freely eat the fruit of every tree in the garden—* ***17*** *except the tree of the knowledge of good and evil. If you eat its fruit, you are sure to die.""*
>
> (Genesis 2:8-9, 15-16)

In the next chapter the serpent, which the Bible later identifies as Satan, comes to tempt Eve.[33]

> *"The serpent was the shrewdest of all the wild animals the LORD God had made. One day he asked the woman, "Did God really say you must not eat the fruit from any of the trees in the garden?" "Of course we may eat fruit from the trees in the garden," the woman replied.* ***3*** *"It's only the fruit from the tree in the middle of the garden that we are not allowed to eat. God said, 'You must not eat it or even touch it; if you do, you will die.'"* ***4*** *"You won't die!" the serpent replied to the woman.* ***5*** *"God knows that your eyes will be opened as soon as you eat it, and you will be like God, knowing both good and evil.""*
>
> (Genesis 3:1-5)

When the serpent asks Eve, "*Did God really say you must not eat the fruit from any of the trees in the garden*?" what is he doing? He is trying to get Eve to doubt God. He goes on to tell her that God lied to them about the fruit and that they won't die if they eat it. At the heart of this lie is the message that God is untrustworthy. God is not really good. He's not in this relationship for your best interests. He is in this relationship for himself because he is selfish.

This is the lie.

What is Eve's response? Eve can look around at the garden and see all the good gifts God has given her and choose to say, *I trust you God because you are good and I want to obey you*. Or she can look to the serpent, believe his words, and say, *I don't trust you God because you aren't good and I want to do what I think is best for myself.* Eve has to make a choice, and she chooses to believe the lie.

> *"The woman was convinced. She saw that the tree was beautiful and its fruit looked delicious, and she wanted the wisdom it would give her. So she took some of the fruit and ate it."*
>
> (Genesis 3:6a)

Here we witness the breaking of the dance God had initiated with humanity. Rather than choosing to love and serve God by obeying his command, Eve chooses to shift the focus of the dance on herself. She steps away from giving God glory towards what she believes will provide herself with glory. Eve then offers Adam the fruit.

> *"Then she gave some to her husband, who was with her . . ."*
>
> (Genesis 3:6b)

Did you catch that? Adam was standing right next to her! He watches Eve eat the fruit. Rather than fighting for and rescuing her from the situation, he watches his wife kill herself.

Now that Eve has taken the fruit, Adam must make a choice. Does he turn his back on Eve by rejecting the fruit and continue following God, or does he turn his back on God and follow Eve in death. It's a painful choice. Does he choose God or does he choose his bride? Finishing the verse we read that Adam takes the fruit.

In a sense, by eating the fruit Adam is saying to Eve, "*I love you so much that if we can't be together, I will choose death rather than living without you.*" In a crazy sense, it's almost as if Adam allows Eve to take the fruit *so that* he can show her the depths of his love. But who is the first casualty of this love affair?

God.

God invites Eve into the dance of his love and she responds by slapping him in the face. She breaks the dance by believing Satan's lie that God is a selfish liar by eating the forbidden fruit in hope of glorifying herself.

Eve chooses herself over God.

Likewise, God invites Adam into the dance and he responds by having an affair. Adam breaks the dance by believing Eve to be more important than his relationship with God. He decides that abandoning God is a necessary cost to love Eve.

Adam chooses Eve over God.

> *"At that moment their eyes were opened, and they suddenly felt shame at their nakedness. So they sewed fig leaves together to cover themselves."*
>
> (Genesis 3:7)

Now we see the effects of sin. After Adam and Eve took the fruit, something changed in their hearts. Self-giving love was no longer natural for them. Their hearts were now infested with selfishness. From this point on, choosing selfless love would be a battle. Suddenly Adam and Eve see the other's body as something to take advantage of. As selfishness crashes in on their marriage they feel compelled to make clothes to cover their nakedness. They begin to hide themselves physically and emotionally. There is no longer the sense of perfect safety and honesty between them. What was once innocent and pure has been tainted.

Sin means "to miss the mark."[34] Tim Keller writes, "Sin is looking to something else besides God for your salvation."[35] When we seek ultimate satisfaction, purpose or meaning in life from anything besides God, we miss the mark. Adam and Eve missed the mark and we continue to see the consequences of their choice in the world today.

> *"When the cool evening breezes were blowing, the man and his wife heard the Lord God walking about in the garden. So they hid from the Lord God among the trees.*
> ***9*** *Then the Lord God called to the man, "Where are you?"*
> ***10*** *He replied, "I heard you walking in the garden, so I hid. I was afraid because I was naked."*
> ***11*** *"Who told you that you were naked?" the Lord God asked. "Have you eaten from the tree whose fruit I commanded you not to eat?"*
> ***12*** *The man replied, "It was the woman you gave me who gave me the fruit, and I ate it."*
> ***13*** *Then the Lord God asked the woman, "What have you done?" "The serpent deceived me," she replied. "That's why I ate it.""*
>
> (Genesis 3:8-13)

Rather than taking responsibility for their actions, Adam and Eve shift blame. Adam dumps the responsibility on Eve. He doesn't man up and Eve follows his sad example by shifting blame to the serpent. Can you see how this conversation must have broken God's heart? The beings created in his image have missed the mark.

> *"And the LORD God made clothing from animal skins for Adam and his wife."*
>
> (Genesis 3:21)

Notice that God doesn't force them to take off their fig leaves and act like everything is alright. He provides them with proper clothes. By giving them clothes, God affirms that something fundamental about their hearts has changed. He also kills an animal, an *innocent* animal. God is showing them that it is only through the shedding of innocent blood that their sin and shame will be covered.

From the Ashes of Eden

Think about this for a minute. Isn't it amazing that God didn't strike Adam and Eve dead on the spot? They both turned their backs on him, and they are still alive? Is there no greater injustice than to betray a God of perfect love? But God spares Adam and Eve. He shows them mercy and kills an animal in their place to show them what they deserve and uses the skins to clothe them. What a profound response from God. Despite their deep betrayal, he lets them live and continues to provide for them.

> *"Then the Lord God said, "Look, the human beings have become like us, knowing both good and evil. What if they reach out, take fruit from the tree of life, and eat it? Then they will live forever!"* **23** *So the Lord God banished them from the Garden of Eden, and he sent Adam out to cultivate the ground from which he had been made.* **24** *After sending them out, the Lord God stationed mighty cherubim to the east of the Garden of Eden. And he placed a flaming sword that flashed back and forth to guard the way to the tree of life."*
>
> (Genesis 3:22-24)

Why is God concerned that they will eat from the tree of life and live forever? God is actually working for their good. He sees the sickness of the sin that has taken root in their hearts and knows how cruel it would be to allow humanity to stay trapped in their sinful state. Rather than allowing man to live under the curse of sin, he causes Adam and Eve to leave the garden.

At the end of Genesis chapter 2 everything seems to be going marvellously. Then, less than a chapter later it appears the entire story has turned into chaos. *So what was God thinking when he created the tree of the knowledge of good and evil?* If he knew this disaster was going to unfold, why plant the tree? Why create Adam and Eve in the first place? Instead of Adam and Eve, God could have created Bob and Jane and programmed them to faithfully obey him and they would still be living in the garden today.

Let's start with the tree. God could have easily placed Adam and Eve in the garden without the tree. He could have created it so that there was no possible way for them to disobey him. But what is love if we have no choice? In the film *The Stepford Wives* a bunch of men in a town turn their wives into robots that are programmed to meet their every need. Do you think it was loving for the husbands to take away their wives' free will by turning them into machines, even if they were programmed to *feel* happy?

God created us in his image and gave us the ability to choose because *true* love is always a choice. Love requires vulnerability and self-sacrifice. God did not want to force his love on humanity; he wanted humanity to experience the highest form of love; love that is freely given; *his* kind of love. And to do that God had to give humanity the option to reject his love. He had to create the tree.

Why then didn't God create two people with freewill who would not have turned against him? Why would God create us if he knew we would reject him? Imagine you meet someone and begin falling in love. Somehow you have been given the ability to look into the future and you see that after giving your heart to this person they will abandon you. I doubt many people placed in this hypothetical scenario would pursue a relationship that they know will cause them tremendous pain.

But what would someone do if their heart was motivated by perfect love? Perfect love would gladly suffer the pain of rejection for the chance of being with the other. In fact, being rejected would present an opportunity to demonstrate the purity of one's love by continuing the pursuit *despite* the other's rejection. This gives us a hint as to why God created Adam and Eve. He knew they would abandon him, but he would use the greatest act of betrayal to demonstrate the greatest act of love. It was all part of his plan. From the ashes of Eden, God was planning to transform a tragedy into the greatest love story of all time.

Key Points:

- God is triune: one in essence, three in person. Self-giving love and relationship is at the core of his being.
- We are created in God's image which means we were built for relationship.
- God did not create humans because he was lonely or needed our worship to feel good about himself. God created mankind so that we could experience his love.
- Both genders are equal and reveal something distinct about the heart of God.
- The covenant of marriage is a picture of the Trinity's unbreakable relationship. This means marriage is a sacred institution that is about serving the other person and, by doing so, directing glory to God.
- God kills an animal and uses the skin to give Adam and Eve clothes. God does this to show them that it is only through the shedding of innocent blood that their shame will be covered.

THREE

JOURNEY TO A NEW BEGINNING

BY THE TIME we reach Genesis chapter 12, almost 2000 years have passed since Adam and Eve were cast out of the garden and humans have spread across the earth along with their corruption. We find that God comes to a man named Abram and tells him to embark on an adventure.

> *"The LORD had said to Abram, "Leave your native country, your relatives, and your father's family, and go to the land that I will show you.* ***2*** *I will make you into a great nation. I will bless you and make you famous, and you will be a blessing to others.* ***3*** *I will bless those who bless you and curse those who treat you with contempt. All the families on earth will be blessed through you."* ***4*** *So Abram departed as the LORD had instructed, and Lot went with him. Abram was seventy-five years old when he left Haran.* ***5*** *He took his wife, Sarai, his*

nephew Lot, and all his wealth—his livestock and all the people he had taken into his household at Haran—and headed for the land of Canaan."

(Genesis 12:1-5a)

God tells Abram that he will make him into a great nation that will be a blessing to the entire world. Wow, this is amazing! Clearly God is up to something by making this promise, but why choose this man Abram? Did God just draw his name out of a hat? If we look at the previous chapter, Genesis 11, we may find clues as to why God made his selection.

"At one time all the people of the world spoke the same language and used the same words. **2** *As the people migrated to the east, they found a plain in the land of Babylonia and settled there.* **3** *They began saying to each other, "Let's make bricks and harden them with fire." (In this region bricks were used instead of stone, and tar was used for mortar.)* **4** *Then they said, "Come, let's build a great city for ourselves with a tower that reaches into the sky. This will make us famous and keep us from being scattered all over the world."* **5** *But the LORD came down to look at the city and the tower the people were building.* **6** *"Look!" he said. "The people are united, and they all speak the same language. After this, nothing they set out to do will be impossible for them!* **7** *Come, let's go down and confuse the people with different languages. Then they won't be able to understand each other."* **8** *In that way, the LORD scattered them all over the world, and they stopped building the city.* **9** *That is why the city was*

called Babel, because that is where the LORD confused the people with different languages. In this way he scattered them all over the world."

(Genesis 11:1-9)

The tower builders declare the reason for their project is to make their names famous. The goal is to glorify themselves. God's desire has always been to share his perfect self-giving love with humanity, yet the tower builder's motivation for their project is self-glorification. It's a deadly counterfeit to God's love and the same self-centered love that corrupted humanity in the garden. Foreseeing the evil that will be caused by mankind coming together in this way, God confuses their speech so that the people scatter.

At the end of Chapter 11 we are introduced to Abram and his family.

"This is the account of Terah's family. Terah was the father of Abram, Nahor, and Haran; and Haran was the father of Lot. ***28*** *But Haran died in Ur of the Chaldeans, the land of his birth, while his father, Terah, was still living.* ***29*** *Meanwhile, Abram and Nahor both married. The name of Abram's wife was Sarai, and the name of Nahor's wife was Milcah. (Milcah and her sister Iscah were daughters of Nahor's brother Haran.)* ***30*** *But Sarai was unable to become pregnant and had no children."*

(Genesis 11:27-30)

Why does the Bible tell us this information? This part of the story almost feels like filler and it's easy to quickly skim over. However, if we take a deeper look at the text, we may find something interesting. Let's summarise what we are told.

Abram's father Terah has three sons: Abram, Nahor and Haran.

Haran has one son, Lot, and two daughters: Milcah and Iscah.

Haran dies young.

Nahor marries his niece, Milcah, and Abram marries someone named Sarai.

Sarai cannot have children.

Which of these points catches your attention? How about Abram's brother Nahor marrying his niece Milcah? Why would Nahor do this? There is a verse in a later book in the Bible called Deuteronomy that might give us an idea of what is going on.

> *"If two brothers are living together on the same property and one of them dies without a son, his widow may not be married to anyone from outside the family. Instead, her husband's brother should marry her and have intercourse with her to fulfill the duties of a brother-in-law.* ***6*** *The first son she bears to him will be considered the son of the dead brother, so that his name will not be forgotten in Israel."*
>
> (Deuteronomy 25:5-6)

This practice is known as *yibbum* or levirate marriage and was instituted by God after the time of Abram. That said, the situation with Nahor looks somewhat similar to the practice outlined in Deuteronomy. The point of yibbum is to carry on the name of one's dead brother "so that his name will not be forgotten." When Haran died, his family was left behind. By marrying his niece, it's almost as if Nahor is stepping in to make sure his brother's daughter is cared and provided for. He is also acting to personally carry on his brother's legacy by keeping Milcah in the family. When viewed in these terms, Nahor's actions seem very honourable.

That's all great for Milcah, but what about Haron's other daughter, Iscah? What's fascinating is that Jewish tradition states that Iscah is the same person as Sarai, Abram's wife.[36] [37] If this is true, it means Abram and Nahor each married one of their nieces. So how does any of this connect to why God might have chosen Abram?

Think back to the reason the people were building the tower. They were building it to make *their* names famous. Contrast that with Abram who takes his brother's daughter as a wife to ensure that his brother's name and legacy survives. The tower builders seek their own glory while Abram seeks his brother's glory. Perhaps this is why God chooses to bless Abram as the father of the nation of Israel. Could it be that God sees Abram living to make his brother's name famous and concludes that this is the person he wants to use to make *his* name famous in the world?

Then we discover something terrible. Sarai can't have children. To the ancient Jews, barrenness was considered to be a sign of God's disfavour. Without a male heir, a relative or someone from outside your family would be appointed to take over your estate. Children were also there to care for you in your old age and carry on your name once you died. What does Sarai's infertility mean for Abram? It means that not only will he not be able to carry on his brother's legacy, but he is unable to carry on his *own* name. If he is to remain faithful to Sarai, he will die in a disgraced state of childlessness.

Flight to the Well

In Genesis 12, God promises to make Abram into a great nation, but there is a problem. How is God going to make Abram into a great nation if his wife is barren? Time passes and Sarai continues to remain childless. Finally, in Genesis 15, Abram confronts God about this predicament.

> *"Some time later, the Lord spoke to Abram in a vision and said to him, "Do not be afraid, Abram, for I will protect you, and your reward will be great."* **2** *But Abram replied, "O Sovereign Lord, what good are all your blessings when I don't even have a son? Since you've given me no children, Eliezer of Damascus, a servant in my household, will inherit all my wealth.* **3** *You have given me no descendants of my own, so one of my servants will be my heir."* **4** *Then the Lord said to him, "No, your servant will not be your heir, for you will have a son of your own who will be your heir."* **5** *Then the Lord took Abram outside and said to him, "Look up into the sky and count the stars if you can. That's how many descendants you will have!"* **6** *And Abram believed the Lord, and the Lord counted him as righteous because of his faith."*
>
> (Genesis 15:1-6)

God promises Abram a son. Yet despite this pledge, time continues to pass with no sign of a child. Losing faith, Sarai decides to implement plan B.

> *"Now Sarai, Abram's wife, had not been able to bear children for him. But she had an Egyptian servant named Hagar.* ***2*** *So Sarai said to Abram, "The Lord has prevented me from having children. Go and sleep with my servant. Perhaps I can have children through her.""*
>
> (Genesis 16:1-2)

Sarai encourages Abram to engage in a custom of the time in which she offers her husband one of her servants to produce an heir. But look at Sarai's logic. If she really believed that God is the one preventing her from having children, why is she trying to go behind God's back to get a child through her servant?

Abram decides to go ahead with Sarai's suggestion without asking for God's input and the plan ends up causing a disaster. Sarai's servant Hagar becomes pregnant and a nasty rivalry grips the two women. The relationship becomes so unbearable that Hagar runs away.

The story continues when a character called the *angel of the LORD* finds Hagar in the wilderness.

> *"The angel of the Lord found Hagar beside a spring of water in the wilderness, along the road to Shur.* ***8*** *The angel said to her, "Hagar, Sarai's servant, where have you come from, and where are you going?" "I'm running away from my mistress, Sarai," she replied.* ***9*** *The angel of the Lord said to her, "Return to your mistress, and submit to her authority."* ***10*** *Then he added, "I will give you more descendants than you can count."*
> ***11*** *And the angel also said, "You are now pregnant and*

will give birth to a son. You are to name him Ishmael (which means 'God hears'), for the Lord has heard your cry of distress. ***12*** *This son of yours will be a wild man, as untamed as a wild donkey! He will raise his fist against everyone, and everyone will be against him. Yes, he will live in open hostility against all his relatives."* ***13*** *Thereafter, Hagar used another name to refer to the Lord, who had spoken to her. She said, "You are the God who sees me." She also said, "Have I truly seen the One who sees me?"* ***14*** *So that well was named Beer-lahai-roi (which means "well of the Living One who sees me"). It can still be found between Kadesh and Bered."*

(Genesis 16:7-14)

This is the first time we hear of an angel appearing to someone in the Bible. What is intriguing is that many scholars believe that this angel, known as *the angel of the LORD* in this chapter, is the first appearance of God the Son in the Bible, the second member of the Trinity.[38]

Okay, all of a sudden this passage got interesting. Why would God the Son choose this passage to first reveal himself in physical form? Examining the text, another unique feature stands out. This is the first time a well is spoken of in the Bible.[39]

Hints of the Plan

"So Hagar gave Abram a son, and Abram named him Ishmael. ***16*** *Abram was eighty-six years old when Ishmael was born.* ***1*** *When Abram was ninety-nine*

years old, the L*ORD* *appeared to him and said, "I am El-Shaddai—'God Almighty.' Serve me faithfully and live a blameless life.* **2** *I will make a covenant with you, by which I will guarantee to give you countless descendants."* **3** *At this, Abram fell face down on the ground. Then God said to him,* **4** *"This is my covenant with you: I will make you the father of a multitude of nations!* **5** *What's more, I am changing your name. It will no longer be Abram. Instead, you will be called Abraham, for you will be the father of many nations.""*

(Genesis 16:15-17:5)

God changes Abram's name from "exalted father" to mean "father of many."[40] This is God's way of telling Abram that he is already seen as the father of many nations despite only having one son. Now, wherever Abraham goes and when anyone calls his name, he will be reminded of God's promise.

""I will make you extremely fruitful. Your descendants will become many nations, and kings will be among them! **7** *I will confirm my covenant with you and your descendants after you, from generation to generation. This is the everlasting covenant: I will always be your God and the God of your descendants after you.* **8** *And I will give the entire land of Canaan, where you now live as a foreigner, to you and your descendants. It will be their possession forever, and I will be their God.""*

(Genesis 17:6-8)

A few verses later God also changes Sarai's name.

> *"Then God said to Abraham, "Regarding Sarai, your wife—her name will no longer be Sarai. From now on her name will be Sarah.""*
>
> (Genesis 17:15)

Sarai means "my princess." God changes her name from "my princess" to Sarah, which means "the princess of a multitude." [41] By changing Sarai's name as well, God is signifying that his covenant with Abraham will come through Sarah.

> *""And I will bless her and give you a son from her! Yes, I will bless her richly, and she will become the mother of many nations. Kings of nations will be among her descendants." **17** Then Abraham bowed down to the ground, but he laughed to himself in disbelief. "How could I become a father at the age of 100?" he thought. "And how can Sarah have a baby when she is ninety years old?" **18** So Abraham said to God, "May Ishmael live under your special blessing!" **19** But God replied, "No—Sarah, your wife, will give birth to a son for you. You will name him Isaac, and I will confirm my covenant with him and his descendants as an everlasting covenant. **20** As for Ishmael, I will bless him also, just as you have asked. I will make him extremely fruitful and multiply his descendants. He will become the father of twelve princes, and I will make him a great nation. **21** But my covenant will be confirmed with Isaac, who will be born to you and Sarah about this time next year.""*
>
> (Genesis 17:19-21)

God promises a miracle child that will be born to Sarah

and it is through this child that God will confirm an everlasting covenant. The words everlasting covenant should tip us off that God is orchestrating something big here. Notice that after God tells Abraham that Sarah will have a son, he laughs. Then, as if to affirm how stunning the news of this covenant child really is, God tells Abraham to name the boy "laughter".[42]

As a mark of this covenant, God tells Abraham to do something.

> *""This is the covenant that you and your descendants must keep: Each male among you must be circumcised.*
> ***11*** *You must cut off the flesh of your foreskin as a sign of the covenant between me and you.* ***12*** *From generation to generation, every male child must be circumcised on the eighth day after his birth. This applies not only to members of your family but also to the servants born in your household and the foreign-born servants whom you have purchased.* ***13*** *All must be circumcised. Your bodies will bear the mark of my everlasting covenant.* ***14*** *Any male who fails to be circumcised will be cut off from the covenant family for breaking the covenant.""*
>
> (Genesis 17:10-14)

Hold up.

What is God thinking?! This is straight-up weird not to mention painful. Why does God choose circumcision as the sign of this "everlasting covenant"? The common explanation is that the foreskin is a picture of sin. Abraham and his descendants were to cut themselves off from sin because they were to show the world what it looked like to live in right relationship with God.

Alright, so God's point is that he wants Abraham's descendants to cut themselves off from sin, but still, why the foreskin? There is a strange phrase used of circumcision later in the Bible that may give us a clue. On multiple occasions, the Bible talks about circumcising the heart.[43] One such example is in Deuteronomy 30:6 where a prophecy is given about the future of the nation Israel.

> *"And the Lord your God will circumcise your heart and the heart of your offspring, so that you will love the Lord your God with all your heart and with all your soul, that you may live."*
>
> (Deuteronomy 30:6)[44]

When Adam and Eve sinned in the garden, their hearts became tainted with selfishness and the dance of love that God had invited them into was broken. Here God is speaking of a time where their hearts will be cut off from sin and restored to the original state they once had in the garden.

God is explicitly saying that sin is a heart issue. Like a lethal virus, sin has spread to the very core of who we are. The only way to restore the relationship we had with God in Eden is for God to circumcise our hearts. Notice that the verse does not say that *we* will circumcise our heart, but God will. It's going to take a divine intervention to rid our hearts of sin. The covenant of circumcision with Abraham is a picture and a reminder of a coming time when God himself will remove sin to restore relationship with mankind.

If this is the meaning of circumcision then perhaps we

can better understand why God chose this sign. What was the first thing that happened when sin entered the world in Genesis chapter three? Adam and Eve realized that they were naked and made clothes from fig leaves to cover themselves. The innocence of nakedness was lost and they experienced shame. Clothes are a constant reminder that something has gone wrong in our hearts. Interestingly, circumcision deals with the most personal and private part of the male body; the same part that is hidden because of shame. By cutting away the foreskin, the most sensitive part of a man is completely exposed. In a sense, a man's clothing is stripped off and he is left naked.

This is an allusion to the garden.

The sign is pointing to a time when God will strip our hearts of sin and our once pure relationship with him and each other will be restored. Yet this process of restoration also involves great pain. There is a price. God is saying that the process of cutting away sin will not be easy or fun. It will be a sacrifice.

Notice that God does not instruct women to undergo any circumcision-like act. This was because the women were counted as bearing the sign through the representation of the males in the nation.[45] It's as if God is sending a message to the men that they are the ones responsible for dealing with sin in their families. If the men do not deal with the sin, the women are stuck. It's almost like God is setting a standard for the men by saying, I want you to live your lives so opposed to sin that you will go to the extreme of cutting off your foreskin to cover your wives and daughters from the curse of sin. With the man embracing this responsibility, there is an echo of the radical self-giving love of God. Rather than standing passively and watching Eve take from the tree, God commands the men to take action. They are to do whatever it takes to save Eve.

Circumcision was a constant reminder to a man of God's covenant plan because he carried the wound on his own body, but what about women? Women would see the covenant sign in marriage. Each time a husband and wife came together intimately they would see the covenant mark. Today we find nudity in infants, vice and marriage. In infants there is an innocence and unawareness of nudity. In vice, pornography or sexual relationships outside of God's plan, there is a sense of lost innocence with an awareness of nudity. But within marriage there is both a sense of innocence and awareness of nudity in the presence of another. This means that when a husband and wife come together, naked and unashamed, they are acting out a picture of what it was like in the garden. They get to imitate and experience a picture of the love and joy of the Trinity.

Tim and Kathy Keller write that sex is, "the most ecstatic, breathtaking, daring, scarcely-to-be-imagined look at the glory that is our future," and it is in the middle of this amazing experience that God places the sign of the everlasting covenant. [46] Circumcision points to God's plan to restore our hearts to a sinless state in the garden where we will live openly and unashamed in God's presence. A time is coming when the open and intimate connection between God and man that was lost in the garden will be restored.

If the union between husband and wife gives us a small look into the excitement, joy, mystery and pleasure of the relationship God desires for us to enjoy, and circumcision is a sign of the covenant that points towards God's plan to redeem mankind, what is the covenant? What was it that God specifically promised?

In Genesis 17 God promises Abraham countless descendants (verse 2), that he will be the father of a multitude of nations (verse 4), that he will be fruitful and kings will be among his descendants (verse 6), that God will be the God of Abraham's descendants, that the covenant will last forever (verse 7), that the land of Canaan will be given to his family (verse 8) and a miracle child will be born to Sarah through whom the covenant will be established forever (verse 19). These are some absolutely astounding blessings God gives to Abraham. He is showing Abraham a picture of his grace.

While the covenant with Abraham is impressive, what does blessing Abraham have to do with God's plan for redeeming the world from sin? The first hint of a connection to God's plan is in the eternal nature of the covenant. We know this covenant is significant because it's everlasting. Secondly, God blesses Abraham beyond his wildest dreams by showing him radical grace. Simply put, grace is unmerited favor. Nothing Abraham ever did, or could do, would merit him receiving these amazing gifts from God. God's plan of redemption will involve pain (circumcision) but also radical grace.

The next hint we receive is in the person God says he will establish the covenant with. It is not Ishmael, Abraham's son with Hagar, but a miracle child God will provide through Sarah. God says, "You will name him Isaac, and I will confirm my covenant with him and his descendants as an everlasting covenant."[47] What is special about this child and how does he fit in God's plan to restore our hearts from sin? More clues await us in the following chapter.

Key Points:

- God makes an everlasting covenant with Abraham and promises a miracle child to be born to Sarah who will confirm the covenant.
- God gives Abraham circumcision as a sign of this covenant which is symbolic of cutting off sin. It also points to God's plan to redeem humanity from sin and restore the relationship he initiated in the garden.

FOUR

MYSTERIES IN THE DESERT

IN GENESIS 21 God's promise to give Abraham and Sarah a son comes to pass.

"The Lord kept his word and did for Sarah exactly what he had promised. **2** *She became pregnant, and she gave birth to a son for Abraham in his old age. This happened at just the time God had said it would.* **3** *And Abraham named their son Isaac.* **4** *Eight days after Isaac was born, Abraham circumcised him as God had commanded.* **5** *Abraham was 100 years old when Isaac was born.* **6** *And Sarah declared, "God has brought me laughter. All who hear about this will laugh with me.* **7** *Who would have said to Abraham that Sarah would nurse a baby? Yet I have given Abraham a son in his old age!""*

(Genesis 21:1-7)

As the chapter continues, Sarah tells Abraham to cast out Hagar and Ishmael from the family on the grounds that Ishmael may become the future heir of the estate rather than Isaac. Sarah says to Abraham,

> *"Cast out this slave woman with her son, for the son of this slave woman shall not be heir with my son Isaac."*
>
> (Genesis 21:10) [48]

This demand causes Abraham great distress but God tells him to listen to his wife.

> *"But God told Abraham, "Do not be upset over the boy and your servant. Do whatever Sarah tells you, for Isaac is the son through whom your descendants will be counted.* ***13*** *But I will also make a nation of the descendants of Hagar's son because he is your son, too."""*
>
> (Genesis 21:12-13)[49]

So what happens to Hagar? Continuing the story,

> *"So Abraham got up early the next morning, prepared food and a container of water, and strapped them on Hagar's shoulders. Then he sent her away with their son, and she wandered aimlessly in the wilderness of Beersheba.* ***15*** *When the water was gone, she put the boy in the shade of a bush.* ***16*** *Then she went and*

sat down by herself about a hundred yards away. "I don't want to watch the boy die," she said, as she burst into tears."

(Genesis 21:14-16)

At this point things are looking bleak for Hagar. Her son seems to be dying and she is lost in the wilderness. Will God intervene?

"But God heard the boy crying, and the angel of God called to Hagar from heaven, "Hagar, what's wrong? Do not be afraid! God has heard the boy crying as he lies there. ***18*** *Go to him and comfort him, for I will make a great nation from his descendants."* ***19*** *Then God opened Hagar's eyes, and she saw a well full of water. She quickly filled her water container and gave the boy a drink."*

(Genesis 21:17-19)

In addition to rescuing them from death, God reminds Hagar of the promise he made to her in Genesis 16:10 to greatly multiply Ishmael's descendants. And how does he save them? He open's Hagar's eyes to see a well.

The Sacrifice

As Genesis chapter 21 comes to a close, the stage is set for God to make the ultimate request of Abraham. With Hagar and Ishmael gone, Abraham is left with one son, Isaac; the miracle child God provided through Sarah. The incredible promises God has made with Abraham now rest on the life of this one son. Then God asks Abraham to do the unthinkable.

> *"Some time later, God tested Abraham's faith. "Abraham!" God called. "Yes," he replied. "Here I am."*
> ***2*** *"Take your son, your only son—yes, Isaac, whom you love so much—and go to the land of Moriah. Go and sacrifice him as a burnt offering on one of the mountains, which I will show you.""*
>
> (Genesis 22:1-2)

Excuse me? This idea seems outrageous! God specifically told Abraham that the everlasting covenant would be confirmed with Isaac. How is God supposed to keep his promises to Abraham if Isaac is dead?

Notice that God recognizes Isaac as Abraham's *only* son and the son he loves. This happens to be the first time the word *love* is recorded in the Bible. Everything about God's request screams at Abraham to disobey or, at the very least, negotiate. What is Abraham's response?

> *"The next morning Abraham got up early. He saddled his donkey and took two of his servants with him, along with his son, Isaac. Then he chopped wood for a fire for a burnt offering and set out for the place God had told him about."*
>
> (Genesis 22:3)

What an astounding reaction! There is no record of a

complaint or a plea for a few days to think things over. The next morning Abraham saddles up and leaves with Isaac.

> *"On the third day of their journey, Abraham looked up and saw the place in the distance.* ***5*** *"Stay here with the donkey," Abraham told the servants. "The boy and I will travel a little farther. We will worship there, and then we will come right back.""*
>
> (Genesis 22:4-5)

Why does Abraham tell his servants they are coming back if he plans to sacrifice Isaac? The apparent explanation is that Abraham believes God will raise Isaac from the dead because this is the only way God can keep his promise.[50]

> *"And Abraham took the wood of the burnt offering and laid it on Isaac his son. And he took in his hand the fire and the knife. So they went both of them together. 7 And Isaac said to his father Abraham, "My father!" And he said, "Here I am, my son." He said, "Behold, the fire and the wood, but where is the lamb for a burnt offering?"* ***8*** *Abraham said, "God will provide for himself the lamb for a burnt offering, my son." So they went both of them together."*
>
> (Genesis 22:6-8)[51]

This is the only conversation recorded between Abraham and Isaac. When Isaac asks his father where the sacrifice is, Abraham gives an interesting response saying, "God will provide for himself the lamb for a burnt offering, my son."

Notice first that Abraham says *God himself* will provide the lamb for the sacrifice. Second, Abraham's words can be interpreted by Isaac in two ways. The first way is the way the text is written with the comma at the end.

"God will provide for himself the lamb for a burnt offering, my son."

But notice how the meaning changes if the comma is replaced by a colon.

"God will provide for himself the lamb for a burnt offering: my son."

Abraham seems to be giving an answer that is purposely vague. Will God provide a substitute lamb or will Isaac be the lamb?

Also note that before this conversation in verse six, it says that Abraham and Isaac walked together. There is a sense of oneness in purpose and unity as they go up the mountain. After this conversation with Abraham, it is likely the reality of the situation begins to dawn on Isaac. Yet we see this same phrase again, "*So they went both of them together.*" Despite the perilous situation, Isaac continues to walk in unity with his father.

> *"When they arrived at the place where God had told him to go, Abraham built an altar and arranged the wood on it. Then he tied his son, Isaac, and laid him on the altar on top of the wood."*
>
> (Genesis 22:9)

Many people picture Isaac as a small boy, but scholars believe he was in his mid-twenties to thirties.[52] Do you think there is any chance an old guy like Abraham could resist Isaac?

No way.

This means Isaac *willingly* allowed his father to place him on the altar for sacrifice. Isaac's submission to his father is absolutely amazing. He is willing to lay his life down to please his dad.

> *"And Abraham picked up the knife to kill his son*
> *as a sacrifice.* ***11*** *At that moment the angel of*
> *the LORD called to him from heaven, "Abraham!*
> *Abraham!" "Yes," Abraham replied. "Here I am!"*
> ***12*** *"Don't lay a hand on the boy!" the angel said. "Do*
> *not hurt him in any way, for now I know that you*
> *truly fear God. You have not withheld from me even*
> *your son, your only son."* ***13*** *Then Abraham looked up*
> *and saw a ram caught by its horns in a thicket. So he*
> *took the ram and sacrificed it as a burnt offering in*
> *place of his son.* ***14*** *Abraham named the place Yahweh-*
> *Yireh (which means "the LORD will provide"). To this*
> *day, people still use that name as a proverb: "On the*
> *mountain of the LORD it will be provided."* ***15*** *Then*
> *the angel of the LORD called again to Abraham from*
> *heaven.* ***16*** *"This is what the LORD says: Because you*
> *have obeyed me and have not withheld even your son,*
> *your only son, I swear by my own name that* ***17*** *I*
> *will certainly bless you. I will multiply your descen-*
> *dants beyond number, like the stars in the sky and the*
> *sand on the seashore. Your descendants will conquer the*
> *cities of their enemies.* ***18*** *And through your descen-*
> *dants all the nations of the earth will be blessed—all*
> *because you have obeyed me.""*
>
> (Genesis 22:10-18)

God intervenes in the last minute and provides a ram to take Isaac's place. Many scholars agree that the angel of the LORD here is another appearance of God the Son.[53] This is a hint that something going on here is important. This event was not about trying to scare or mentally torture Abraham and Isaac. God was dropping some serious clues about his plan for humanity.

Another fascinating thing we discover in this passage is the name Abraham calls the mountain: *Yahweh-Yireh* which means *the Lord* will provide. Not only did God provide on this mountain, but the LORD *will* provide here once again.

> *"So Abraham returned to his young men, and they arose and went together to Beersheba. And Abraham lived at Beersheba."*
>
> (Genesis 22:19)[54]

In verse 19 there is an important detail missing. Can you spot it? Abraham comes down the mountain, but where is Isaac? The verse reads as if Abraham *did* in fact sacrifice his son. Historically Isaac would have come down with his father before going home, but the fact that the text only speaks of Abraham returning could be a clue.

Finding the Bride

By the time we reach chapter 24, many years have passed and Abraham decides to find a wife for his son. He sends his most senior servant on a journey to find a bride for Isaac. While the servant's name is not recorded here, it is likely this is the same servant Abraham names in Genesis 15:2 as

Eliezer which means "God of Help."[55] We pick up the story with Abraham's servant in verse 10.

> *"Then he loaded ten of Abraham's camels with all kinds of expensive gifts from his master, and he traveled to distant Aram-naharaim. There he went to the town where Abraham's brother Nahor had settled.* ***11*** *He made the camels kneel beside a well just outside the town. It was evening, and the women were coming out to draw water."*
>
> (Genesis 24:10-11)

The servant comes to the well in the evening because this was the time and place where women would come to draw water. Here the servant makes a bold request.

> *""O Lord, God of my master, Abraham," he prayed. "Please give me success today, and show unfailing love to my master, Abraham.* ***13*** *See, I am standing here beside this spring, and the young women of the town are coming out to draw water.* ***14*** *This is my request. I will ask one of them, 'Please give me a drink from your jug.' If she says, 'Yes, have a drink, and I will water your camels, too!'—let her be the one you have selected as Isaac's wife. This is how I will know that you have shown unfailing love to my master.""*
>
> (Genesis 24:12-14)

The plan is to ask a young woman for a drink of water at the well. Then, if she is the one God has chosen, she will not only give him a drink, but will also offer to water his 10 camels. Take a moment to think through this request. The women coming to the well are probably tired from a long day's work. A thirsty camel can drink 30 gallons of water in 13 minutes.[56] Think about how much effort it would take to lower a jar into a well and repeatedly haul it back up to quench the thirst of just *one* camel. In short, you have to be an extraordinary person to freely offer water to a stranger's 10 camels.

> *"Before he had finished praying, he saw a young woman named Rebekah coming out with her water jug on her shoulder. She was the daughter of Bethuel, who was the son of Abraham's brother Nahor and his wife, Milcah.* ***16*** *Rebekah was very beautiful and old enough to be married, but she was still a virgin. She went down to the spring, filled her jug, and came up again."*
>
> (Genesis 24:16-18)

The name Rebekah means "a rope with a noose" which is suggested to signify her beauty which ensnares a man.[57] With this in mind, it has been suggested one translation for her name is "captivating."[58]

> *"Running over to her, the servant said, "Please give me a little drink of water from your jug."* ***18*** *"Yes, my lord," she answered, "have a drink." And she quickly lowered her jug from her shoulder and gave him a drink.* ***19*** *When she had given him a drink, she said, "I'll draw water for your camels, too, until they have*

had enough to drink." ***20*** *So she quickly emptied her jug into the watering trough and ran back to the well to draw water for all his camels."*

(Genesis 24:17-20)

This is amazing. The servant asks for "a little drink" and Rebekah responds by freely offering to spend the rest of her evening watering his entire caravan. She responds with a heart committed to radical self-giving.

"The servant watched her in silence, wondering whether or not the Lord had given him success in his mission. ***22*** *Then at last, when the camels had finished drinking, he took out a gold ring for her nose and two large gold bracelets for her wrists.* ***23*** *"Whose daughter are you?" he asked. "And please tell me, would your father have any room to put us up for the night?"* ***24*** *"I am the daughter of Bethuel," she replied. "My grandparents are Nahor and Milcah.* ***25*** *Yes, we have plenty of straw and feed for the camels, and we have room for guests."* ***26*** *The man bowed low and worshiped the Lord.* ***27*** *"Praise the Lord, the God of my master, Abraham," he said. "The Lord has shown unfailing love and faithfulness to my master, for he has led me straight to my master's relatives."* ***28*** *The young woman ran home to tell her family everything that had happened."*

(Genesis 24:21-28)

Rebekah runs home to share this news with her family and they invite Abraham's servant into their home where they wash his feet and feed him. Here Abraham's servant officially requests to take Rebekah back with him and present her as a bride to his master's son. Rebekah's family replies,

> *""Here is Rebekah; take her and go. Yes, let her*
> *be the wife of your master's son, as the Lord has*
> *directed."* ***52*** *When Abraham's servant heard their*
> *answer, he bowed down to the ground and worshiped*
> *the Lord.* ***53*** *Then he brought out silver and gold jew-*
> *elry and clothing and presented them to Rebekah. He*
> *also gave expensive presents to her brother and mother.*
> ***54*** *Then they ate their meal, and the servant and the*
> *men with him stayed there overnight. But early the next*
> *morning, Abraham's servant said, "Send me back to my*
> *master."* ***55*** *"But we want Rebekah to stay with us at*
> *least ten days," her brother and mother said. "Then she*
> *can go."* ***56*** *But he said, "Don't delay me. The Lord has*
> *made my mission successful; now send me back so I*
> *can return to my master."* ***57*** *"Well," they said, "we'll*
> *call Rebekah and ask her what she thinks."* ***58*** *So they*
> *called Rebekah. "Are you willing to go with this man?"*
> *they asked her. And she replied, "Yes, I will go.""*
>
> (Genesis 24:51-57)

Rebekah agrees to leave with the servant right away to marry a man she has never even seen. In verse 62, Isaac finally reappears in the text. After coming from *the well of the Living One who sees me* named by Hagar in Genesis 16:13, he sees the camels returning with Rebekah. Here the servant presents Rebekah to Isaac and they are married. We also learn in the next chapter that Isaac and Rebekah settle by this well.[59]

The story of Abraham's offering of Isaac on the mountain and the marriage of Isaac to Rebekah are rich with symbolism that points towards God's plan of redemption. However, we need to continue reading if we are to properly understand what the story is pointing to. We will return to these chapters and unpack them once we gather some more puzzle pieces, but for the moment I want to focus on a pattern in Rebekah's betrothal story that we find in other parts of the Bible.

A Cryptic Pattern

There are six features in the story we just read that I want to highlight. First, Abraham's servant is a male who travels to a foreign land. Second, he comes to a well. Third, a woman meets him at the well. Fourth, the woman runs home with a report. Fifth, the man is invited back to the woman's home. Sixth, there is an engagement or marriage.

The second place we see this pattern in the Bible is in a story about Isaac's son Jacob in Genesis 29. In the chapter Jacob arrives in a foreign land (verse 1) and comes to a well (verse 2). A woman comes to the well (verse 6) and runs home with a report (verse 12). Jacob is invited into the woman's home (verse 14) and is betrothed to her (verse 19).

The third story where we find this pattern is in Exodus chapter 2. Exodus is the second book in the Bible and it begins with the people of Israel (Jacob's descendants) living enslaved in Egypt. Moses, a Jewish child adopted by Pharaoh's daughter, is raised as royalty but is forced to flee after murdering an Egyptian who he sees beating a Jewish slave. Once more, we again see this six stage pattern. In verse 15 Moses flees to a foreign land and comes to a well. Several women arrive at the well (verse 16) and run back to their father and tell him how Moses rescued them from being harassed (verse 19). Moses is invited back to their home (verses 19 -20) and this leads to a marriage with one of the daughters (verse 21).

What can we learn from the pattern established in these stories? It appears that when a foreign man meets a woman at a well, a chain of events can be triggered that leads to a marriage. Remember this pattern because it contains a puzzle piece that will help us solve an important passage in the future.

Key Points:

- Both Abraham and Isaac walk up the mountain in unity and Isaac does not resist being sacrificed by his father.
- Abraham names the mountain where Isaac was to be sacrificed "the Lord *will provide.*"
- When a male foreigner meets a woman at a well, a series of events can be triggered that leads to a marriage.

FIVE

THE MARRIAGE CONTRACT

IN THE BOOK of Exodus, God sends Moses back to Egypt to demand that Pharaoh free the Israelites from slavery.[60] After God sends 10 plagues, Pharaoh finally releases the Jews who make their way into the wilderness of Sinai under Moses' leadership. We pick up the story in Exodus chapter 19.

> *"Exactly two months after the Israelites left Egypt, they arrived in the wilderness of Sinai.* **2** *After break-*
> *ing camp at Rephidim, they came to the wilderness of Sinai and set up camp there at the base of Mount*
> *Sinai.* **3** *Then Moses climbed the mountain to appear before God. The* Lord *called to him from the mountain and said, "Give these instructions to the family of Jacob; announce it to the descendants of Israel:* **4** *'You*
> *have seen what I did to the Egyptians. You know how*

I carried you on eagles' wings and brought you to
myself. ***5*** *Now if you will obey me and keep my cov-*
enant, you will be my own special treasure from among
all the peoples on earth; for all the earth belongs to
me. ***6*** *And you will be my kingdom of priests, my holy*
nation.' This is the message you must give to the people
of Israel." ***7*** *So Moses returned from the mountain and*
called together the elders of the people and told them
everything the Lord had commanded him. ***8*** *And all*
the people responded together, "We will do everything
the Lord has commanded." So Moses brought the
people's answer back to the Lord. ***9*** *Then the Lord said*
to Moses, "I will come to you in a thick cloud, Moses,
so the people themselves can hear me when I speak
with you. Then they will always trust you." Moses told
the Lord what the people had said."

(Exodus 19:1-9)

In verse five, God mentions another covenant. This covenant refers to the Ten Commandments which are listed in Exodus 20.[61] The Ten Commandments are a list of laws God gives the nation of Israel:

1. You shall have no other gods before me.
2. You shall not make for yourself a carved image, or any likeness of anything that is in heaven above, or that is in the earth beneath, or that is in the water under the earth.
3. You shall not take the name of the Lord your God in vain.
4. Remember the Sabbath day, to keep it holy.

5. Honor your father and your mother.
6. You shall not murder.
7. You shall not commit adultery.
8. You shall not steal.
9. You shall not bear false witness against your neighbor.
10. You shall not covet.[62]

Could it be that these laws are a marriage contract between God and Israel? At first, this idea sounds strange. What could possibly suggest that the Ten Commandments form a type of marriage contract?[63]

In ancient Israel, a formal wedding contract called the ketubah was used to outline the obligations of the groom to his bride.[64] The word ketubah comes from the Hebrew word *katav* which means "to write." The ketubah is still used in Jewish weddings today and is a legally binding document in Israel.[65] This kind of contract is outlined by God in Exodus.

> *""Now if you will obey me and keep my covenant [the Ten Commandments], you will be my own special treasure from among all the peoples on earth; for all the earth belongs to me.* ***6*** *And you will be my kingdom of priests, my holy nation.' This is the message you must give to the people of Israel.""*
>
> (Exodus 19:5-6)

The Ten Commandments are referred to here as "my covenant."[66] God tells Israel that if they obey him, they will be his special treasure. In addition, he says they will be a kingdom of priests which means that God is honouring Israel with the privilege of accessing his presence.

> *"Then the* Lord *told Moses, "Go down and prepare the people for my arrival. Consecrate them today and tomorrow, and have them wash their clothing.""*
>
> (Exodus 19:10)

This washing sounds like the ritual bath in Judaism called mikveh which was a ceremonial immersion the priests had to undergo before entering God's presence.[67] [68] This washing, like circumcision, symbolized a removing of sin.[69] Interestingly, mikveh is also used as a pre-wedding cleansing by a bride and groom in Judaism.[70]

In chapters 20-23 God gives Moses more laws in addition to the Ten Commandments which he reads to the nation in chapter 24. We pick up the story in Exodus 24:3.

> *"Then Moses went down to the people and repeated all the instructions and regulations the* Lord *had given him. All the people answered with one voice, "We will do everything the* Lord *has commanded."* **4** *Then Moses carefully wrote down all the* Lord*'s instructions. Early the next morning Moses got up and built an altar at the foot of the mountain. He also set up twelve pillars, one for each of the twelve tribes of Israel.* **5** *Then he sent some of the young Israelite men to present burnt offerings and to sacrifice bulls as peace offerings to the* Lord*.* **6** *Moses drained half the blood from these animals into basins. The other half he splattered against the altar.* **7** *Then he took the Book of the Covenant and*

> *read it aloud to the people. Again they all responded, "We will do everything the LORD has commanded. We will obey."* ***8*** *Then Moses took the blood from the basins and splattered it over the people, declaring, "Look, this blood confirms the covenant the LORD has made with you in giving you these instructions."* ***9*** *Then Moses, Aaron, Nadab, Abihu, and the seventy elders of Israel climbed up the mountain.* ***10*** *There they saw the God of Israel. Under his feet there seemed to be a surface of brilliant blue lapis lazuli, as clear as the sky itself.* ***11*** *And though these nobles of Israel gazed upon God, he did not destroy them. In fact, they ate a covenant meal, eating and drinking in his presence!"*
>
> (Exodus 24:3-11)

Israel willingly enters into this covenant with God which is followed by a meal. Similarly, marriage is a covenant made by two people that is followed by a feast. On this passage in Exodus, Brant Pitre writes,

> "From a biblical perspective, a "covenant" was a sacred family bond between persons, establishing between them a permanent and sacred relationship. In the Exodus account of the covenant at Mount Sinai…we see exactly this kind of relationship being inaugurated. By accepting the terms of the relationship (the Ten Commandments), and by offering worship to God in the form of blood sacrifice, the twelve tribes of Israel are established in a mysterious and sacred relationship with God. This relationship is established by Moses's act of throwing the blood of

the sacrifices on the altar (symbolizing God) and on the elders (representing the people). This action symbolizes that the Creator of the world and the twelve tribes of Israel are now in a "flesh and blood" relationship—that is, they are family."[71]

The most compelling testimony that this event represented a marriage comes from the mouth of God. In the book of Jeremiah, God says,

> *""Go and shout this message to Jerusalem. This is what the LORD says: "I remember how eager you were to please me as a young bride long ago, how you loved me and followed me even through the barren wilderness."""*
>
> (Jeremiah 2:2)

This verse refers to the giving of the law at Mount Sinai which is compared to an engagement or wedding.[72]

The prophet Ezekiel also refers to this event using marriage imagery.

> *"And when I passed by again, I saw that you were old enough for love. So I wrapped my cloak around you to cover your nakedness and declared my marriage vows. I made a covenant with you, says the Sovereign LORD, and you became mine."*
>
> (Ezekiel 16:8)[73]

In the book of Isaiah, God and Israel's relationship is compared to a marriage again.

> *"For your Maker is your husband, the* LORD *of hosts is his name; and the Holy One of Israel is your Redeemer, the God of the whole earth he is called."*
>
> (Isaiah 54:5)

There is also a book in the Bible called the Song of Songs which is a love poem written by King Solomon for his bride. In ancient Israel, the Jews forbade anyone to read this book until they were 30 due to its mature content.[74] What is fascinating is that this book is interpreted by Jews as a picture of God's spousal love for the nation.

If God really did initiate a marriage between himself and Israel at Mount Sinai, then the Ten Commandments acts as a type of marriage contract. This dramatically changes how we see these laws. If the Ten Commandments are a marriage contract, would this document be something reasonable you could sign with your spouse?

1. *You shall have no other gods before me*: I will give exclusive loyalty to my spouse.
2. *You shall not make for yourself a carved image (idols)*: I will allow no one to compete with my love for my spouse.
3. *You shall not take the name of the Lord your God in vain*: I will respect my spouse in public and in private.
4. *Remember the Sabbath day, to keep it holy*: I will regularly set aside time to spend with my spouse.
5. *Honor your father and your mother*: I will honour my in-laws as I do my parents.
6. *You shall not murder*: I will not murder my spouse.

7. *You shall not commit adultery*: I will not cheat on my spouse.
8. *You shall not steal*: I will not rob my spouse physically or emotionally.
9. *You shall not bear false witness against your neighbor*: I will speak truthfully of my spouse.
10. *You shall not covet*: I will be content with my spouse.

When viewed in the context of marriage, the Ten Commandments seem like a perfectly reasonable contract to sign.

And here lies the problem.

While it appears *completely* reasonable for two lovers to keep the Ten Commandments between each other, it is an impossible task. We are hopelessly incapable of keeping these principles, even with the one we love, because sin has corrupted our hearts. The Ten Commandments were given by God to expose the deep-rooted corruption in the human soul. God gave the law to show Israel how impossible it is for them to live up to his standards.

If the Israelites violated any of the Ten Commandments, they were required to make an animal sacrifice to atone for their sins. This was a messy, costly and unpleasant process. It is not fun to kill an innocent animal. It's horrible to watch and that's the point. God wants us to see that the result of sin is death. This is why when Adam and Eve sinned, the first thing God does is to kill an innocent animal in their place. If there is any sin in our lives, we deserve death. That is how disgusted God is when he sees evil. Something must die to pay your debt and appease God's wrath.

Many people believe that God will let them into heaven

one day because they have tried to live an honest life and be a good person. They believe that because God is good he will give them a pass. This sounds nice, but would it work in a court of law?

Imagine you murdered someone and on your day of sentence you say to the judge, "Your honour, I am really sorry for what I did but I believe that because you are a good judge you will set me free." What will the judge say? The judge will reply, "You are right, I am a good judge and because I am a good judge I cannot dismiss your crime." It is the judge's goodness that condemns you. Only a corrupt judge would allow evil to go unpunished.

When it comes to the Ten Commandments, whether you take the Lord's name in vain or murder someone, you are equally condemned in God's eyes because he is holy and all sin is repulsive to him. You deserve death, and unless someone else takes your place, God's goodness and justice demands you pay the price.

God gave the Ten Commandments to reveal the sin in our hearts and our desperate need for him. He knows the marriage contract is reasonable and that it is impossible for Israel to keep in their corrupt state. Still, God goes ahead and enters into this marriage with the full knowledge that Israel will betray him.

God wants his people to see their deep need for his divine intervention in their lives. Through this marriage, God is taking another step in his plan to restore humanity to the garden. He unites himself to a nation and invites them to return to the dance. Granted, this relationship is nowhere near the level of intimacy Adam and Eve enjoyed with God in Eden, but it's a movement forward in the process of restoration.

God begins restoring relationship with a nation he knows will reject him. But through it all, behind the scenes, he is working to establish his plan.

Key Points:

- God compares his relationships with Israel to a marriage. Through this intimate relationship, God invites a nation to begin returning to the dance he had initiated with mankind in the garden.
- The giving of The Ten Commandments resembles a marriage contract and was given to show Israel the sinful condition of their hearts and their desperate need for God.
- God is good and he hates evil passionately. All of us have failed his law and deserve death.

SIX

FORESHADOWS

THE BOOK OF Hosea in the Bible opens with a shocking request.

> *"When the* Lord *first began speaking to Israel through Hosea, he said to him, "Go and marry a prostitute, so that some of her children will be conceived in prostitution. This will illustrate how Israel has acted like a prostitute by turning against the* Lord *and worshiping other gods."* ***3*** *So Hosea married Gomer, the daughter of Diblaim, and she became pregnant and gave Hosea a son."*
>
> (Hosea 1:2-3)

God comes to a man named Hosea and calls him to marry a prostitute to show Israel a picture of her adultery. Israel had neglected her marriage covenant, turning her back on God's laws and worshiping idols which caused God enormous grief. Dr. Ravi Zacharias explains God's distress by saying, "When I say I love you and you refuse to love me, I hurt because I have lost something. When God says he loves you and you refuse to love God, God hurts too, not because God has lost something but you have lost something; that is the very perfection of his love."[75] Hosea is called to take an adulterous wife so he can enter into God's suffering and call the people to repentance.

At the time of Hosea's writing, the Jewish people were fractured into two kingdoms: Israel in the north and Judah in the south. In Hosea chapter two God speaks of the betrayal of the northern kingdom.

> *""But now bring charges against Israel—your mother— for she is no longer my wife, and I am no longer her husband. Tell her to remove the prostitute's makeup from her face and the clothing that exposes her breasts... She doesn't realize it was I who gave her everything she has—the grain, the new wine, the olive oil; I even gave her silver and gold. But she gave all my gifts to Baal."* [76]
>
> (Hosea 2:2, 8)

In our culture, most people would file for divorce in the face of such unashamed cheating, yet God does not tell Hosea to divorce his unfaithful wife. Despite Israel's affairs, God intends to pursue his adulterous people. Listen to the incredible words God speaks over Israel after detailing her rejection of him.

> *""But then I will win her back once again. I will lead her into the desert and speak tenderly to her there.* ***15*** *I will return her vineyards to her and transform the Valley*

of Trouble into a gateway of hope. She will give herself to
me there, as she did long ago when she was young, when I
freed her from her captivity in Egypt. ***16*** *When that day*
comes," says the LORD, *"you will call me 'my husband'*
instead of 'my master.' ***17*** *O Israel, I will wipe the many*
names of Baal from your lips, and you will never men-
tion them again. ***18*** *On that day I will make a covenant*
with all the wild animals and the birds of the sky and the
animals that scurry along the ground so they will not harm
you. I will remove all weapons of war from the land, all
swords and bows, so you can live unafraid in peace and
safety. ***19*** *I will make you my wife forever, showing you*
righteousness and justice, unfailing love and compassion.
20 *I will be faithful to you and make you mine, and you*
will finally know me as the LORD."

(Hosea 2:14-20)

God promises that a time is approaching when wars will end and the animals will be at peace with man. Most significantly, Israel will be God's wife forever and will eternally receive God's righteousness and love. God is revealing more of his eternal plan. God is saying that a day is coming when the dance he started in the garden will begin again, and this time it will be more glorious than ever before. The prophet Jeremiah goes on to speak of this restored marriage covenant saying,

""Behold, the days are coming, declares the LORD, *when*
I will make a new covenant with the house of Israel
and the house of Judah, ***32*** *not like the covenant that*
I made with their fathers on the day when I took them

by the hand to bring them out of the land of Egypt, my covenant that they broke, though I was their husband, declares the LORD. ***33*** *For this is the covenant that I will make with the house of Israel after those days, declares the* LORD: *I will put my law within them, and I will write it on their hearts. And I will be their God, and they shall be my people.* ***34*** *And no longer shall each one teach his neighbor and each his brother, saying, 'Know the* LORD,*' for they shall all know me, from the least of them to the greatest, declares the* LORD. *For I will forgive their iniquity, and I will remember their sin no more."'"*

(Jeremiah 31:31-34)[77]

God promises a new covenant that will be superior to the one made at Mt. Sinai. He says that under this new covenant he will write the law on the people's hearts. Does this remind you of another verse we have seen before?

"And the LORD *your God will circumcise your heart and the heart of your offspring, so that you will love the* LORD *your God with all your heart and with all your soul, that you may live."*

(Deuteronomy 30:6)[78]

The Ten Commandments were given at Mt. Sinai to expose the sin that was rooted in Israel's heart, yet God promises in the book of Deuteronomy to personally cut off their sin. Now in Jeremiah 31, God says he will write the law on Israel's hearts. He is saying that a time is coming when he will cleanse Israel from her sin and the Ten Commandments will become the natural desire of their hearts. This idea is also referenced in the book of Ezekiel where God speaks through the prophet saying,

> *"And I will give you a new heart, and I will put a new spirit in you. I will take out your stony, stubborn heart and give you a tender, responsive heart."*
>
> (Ezekiel 36:26)[79]

The Messiah

A significant detail about the prophecy of the new covenant in Jeremiah is that the Jews interpreted this passage to correspond with the times of the Messiah.[80] *Messiah* means "anointed one" and is a person referenced throughout the Old Testament.[81] In the New Testament of the Bible, the Greek word for Messiah is translated as "Christ". The Jews believed the Messiah was a coming prophet, priest and king who would establish God's kingdom in the world.[82] The book of Micah reveals that the Messiah will be born in the town of Bethlehem.

> *"But you, O Bethlehem Ephrathah, are only a small village among all the people of Judah. Yet a ruler of Israel will come from you, one whose origins are from the distant past."*
>
> (Micah 5:2)

Notice the prophet says that the Messiah's origins are

"from the distant past". The King James Version of the Bible translates this phrase "from everlasting." There is a hint here that the coming Messiah is no ordinary man.[83]

Another interesting prophecy is given in Isaiah,

> *"Therefore the Lord himself will give you a sign. Behold, the virgin shall conceive and bear a son, and shall call his name Immanuel."*
>
> (Isaiah 7:14) [84]

God says a virgin will give birth to a son called Immanuel which means "God with us."[85] Could this miracle child be the promised Messiah?

Isaiah 49:6 tells that the Messiah will bring salvation to the world,

> *"He says, "You will do more than restore the people of Israel to me. I will make you a light to the Gentiles, and you will bring my salvation to the ends of the earth.""* [86]

The Gentiles are non-Jewish peoples and here God promises to bring them salvation. If God has promised a new marriage covenant with Israel, is he also opening this marriage to the non-Jews?

In Isaiah 53 we are given more details about the Messiah and clues as to how he will bring salvation to the ends of the earth.

> *"Yet it was our weaknesses he carried; it was our sorrows that weighed him down. And we thought his troubles were a punishment from God, a punishment*

for his own sins! ***5*** *But he was pierced for our rebellion, crushed for our sins. He was beaten so we could be whole. He was whipped so we could be healed.* ***6*** *All of us, like sheep, have strayed away. We have left God's paths to follow our own. Yet the LORD laid on him the sins of us all.* ***7*** *He was oppressed and treated harshly, yet he never said a word. He was led like a lamb to the slaughter. And as a sheep is silent before the shearers, he did not open his mouth."*

(Isaiah 53:4-7)

We find many significant details in this passage. The Messiah will be "pierced" "whipped" and "beaten" to bring atonement from sin and willingly goes to the slaughter like a lamb. Further details of the Messiah's suffering are foretold by King David in the book of Psalms.

"My enemies surround me like a pack of dogs; an evil gang closes in on me. They have pierced my hands and feet. ***17*** *I can count all my bones. My enemies stare at me and gloat.* ***18*** *They divide my garments among themselves and throw dice for my clothing."*

(Psalm 22:16-18)

In Zechariah 12:10 God also references a piercing.

""Then I will pour out a spirit of grace and prayer on the family of David and on the people of Jerusalem. They will look on me whom they have pierced and mourn for

> *him as for an only son. They will grieve bitterly for him as for a firstborn son who has died."'"*

What is stunning about this passage is that God says they will look on "*me whom they have pierced.*" God says that *he* is the one who Israel will pierce. If this piercing is another reference to the piercing of the Messiah that Isaiah and David spoke of, then the implications are astonishing. Could God himself actually be the promised Messiah?

In Isaiah we are shown a great feast which is a picture of what the Jews call the messianic banquet.

> *"On this mountain the LORD Almighty will prepare a feast of rich food for all peoples, a banquet of aged wine—the best of meats and the finest of wines.* ***7*** *On this mountain he will destroy the shroud that enfolds all peoples, the sheet that covers all nations;* ***8*** *he will swallow up death forever. The Sovereign LORD will wipe away the tears from all faces; he will remove his people's disgrace from all the earth. The LORD has spoken."*
>
> (Isaiah 25:6-8)[87]

The Jews understood this banquet as a description of the future messianic age where the Messiah would reign on earth.[88] Interestingly, the Messiah is not mentioned in the passage and it is God himself, "the LORD Almighty," who prepares the feast.

The passage compares the coming age of the Messiah as a great banquet with the best wines and meats. It will be a banquet that "all peoples" are invited to. This speaks of how the Messiah will open the door of salvation to the entire world and fulfill the covenant God gave to Abraham saying "All the families on earth will be blessed through you."[89] At this banquet, God's people will celebrate death being swallowed up forever and there will be no more tears, sorrow or sickness. Jewish tradition came to believe that this passage in Isaiah described a kind of return to the Garden of Eden.[90] The coming feast he is preparing will not simply be a return to Eden, but a return to a *greater* Eden.

This is a picture of God's plan.

Key Points:

- The book of Hosea describes Israel's adultery against God. Despite her betrayal, God promises to make her his "wife forever."
- Isaiah foretells that a virgin will give birth to a child called Immanuel [God with us].
- The Messiah [anointed one], also known as the Christ, was a person the Jews believed would establish God's kingdom in the world.
- The Messiah will be born in a small town called Bethlehem and his origin comes from the distant past.
- The Messiah will bring salvation to the Jews and the world.

SEVEN

THE FATHER'S HEART

WE NOW LEAVE the first section of the Bible, the Old Testament, and enter into the New Testament. It is in the New Testament that God's seemingly mysterious plan to save mankind is revealed. The clues we have gathered in the Old Testament will help us solve what takes place in the New.[91]

Our journey into the New Testament begins in the book of Luke where the angel Gabriel appears to a young virgin named Mary.

> *"In the sixth month of Elizabeth's pregnancy, God sent the angel Gabriel to Nazareth, a village in Galilee,* ***27*** *to a virgin named Mary. She was engaged to be married to a man named Joseph, a descendant of King David.* ***28*** *Gabriel appeared to her and said, "Greetings, favored woman! The Lord is with you!"*
> ***29*** *Confused and disturbed, Mary tried to think what the angel could mean.* ***30*** *"Don't be afraid, Mary,"*

the angel told her, "for you have found favor with
God! ***31*** *You will conceive and give birth to a son, and*
you will name him Jesus. ***32*** *He will be very great and*
will be called the Son of the Most High. The Lord God
will give him the throne of his ancestor David. ***33*** *And*
he will reign over Israel forever; his Kingdom will never
end!" ***34*** *Mary asked the angel, "But how can this hap-*
pen? I am a virgin." ***35*** *The angel replied, "The Holy*
Spirit will come upon you, and the power of the Most
High will overshadow you. So the baby to be born will
be holy, and he will be called the Son of God.""

(Luke 1:26-35)

Having an angel show up with this message would be a lot to take in. The angel tells Mary that she will give birth to a child who will be called the *Son of the Most High* and will reign as king of Israel forever. The name she is to give the child is Jesus, which means "God is salvation."[92] Not only is Mary a virgin, but we discover in the next chapter that she gives birth in Bethlehem. This leads to one conclusion. This child is the promised Messiah.[93]

But not only will this child be the Messiah, he is also someone much greater. Through this birth, God is doing something incredible, something that would have shocked the Jews as it should shock us. Not only will this child be the Messiah, he is God.

God the Son, the second member of the Trinity, is the one born to Mary and named "God is salvation".

Just stop for a second.

God. The eternal, perfect God of the universe leaves heaven to come to earth as a human. This is wild stuff. We could spend the rest of this chapter talking about how ridiculous this is; and God is not born into a wealthy family in a palace but an average working family.

The Son comes to earth to take the role of the Messiah and bring about the promised new covenant. He arrives on a rescue mission to cleanse the world from sin. But it's more than that. He comes as a sacrifice to cement a love story that will stand for eternity. But before we go any further into Jesus' story, there is something crucial that we need to establish.

Jesus comes to earth to show us God's heart. Many people have a distorted picture of God. They see him as a vengeful, angry, distant being that does not care about human affairs. In order to accurately grasp Jesus' mission to establish the new covenant, we need to understand a story he told to describe who God is.

> *""To illustrate the point further, Jesus told them this story: "A man had two sons.* ***12*** *The younger son told his father, 'I want my share of your estate now before you die.'"""*
>
> (Luke 15:11-12a)

This is one of the most horrible things a son could say to his father. The son is essentially saying, "I wish you were dead, Dad, because all I want is your money. Could you just go ahead and sell your stuff and give me *my* money?" The disrespect this son shows to his father is unbelievable. And what is the father's response?

> *""So his father agreed to divide his wealth between his sons.""*
>
> (Luke 15:12b)

The father actually does it! He cashes out and gives the younger son the money.

> *""A few days later this younger son packed all his*
> *belongings and moved to a distant land, and there he*
> *wasted all his money in wild living. About the time his*
> *money ran out, a great famine swept over the land, and*
> *he began to starve.* ***15*** *He persuaded a local farmer to*
> *hire him, and the man sent him into his fields to feed*
> *the pigs.* ***16*** *The young man became so hungry that even*
> *the pods he was feeding the pigs looked good to him.*
> *But no one gave him anything.* ***17*** *When he finally*
> *came to his senses, he said to himself, 'At home even*
> *the hired servants have food enough to spare, and here*
> *I am dying of hunger!* ***18*** *I will go home to my father*
> *and say, "Father, I have sinned against both heaven*
> *and you,* ***19*** *and I am no longer worthy of being called*
> *your son. Please take me on as a hired servant."'* ***20*** *So*
> *he returned home to his father. And while he was still a*
> *long way off, his father saw him coming.""*
>
> (Luke 15:13-20a)

How did the father see his son coming while he was still far off? That father was waiting. He had always been waiting, patiently staring down the road hoping for his son's return.

""Filled with love and compassion, he ran to his son,
embraced him, and kissed him. ***21*** *His son said to him,*
'Father, I have sinned against both heaven and you,
and I am no longer worthy of being called your son'
22 *But his father said to the servants, 'Quick! Bring the finest robe in the house and put it on him. Get a ring for his finger and sandals for his feet.'""*

(Luke 15:20b-22)

The father can't bear for the son to finish his speech. He cuts him off before he can even request to be made a servant and demands the best robe be brought for his son who was probably dressed in rags. He also gives him a ring, a sign of wealth, dignity and honor, and the most expensive pair of sandals, things that were definitely not worn by servants. [94]

""And kill the calf we have been fattening. We must celebrate with a feast, ***24*** *for this son of mine was dead and has now returned to life. He was lost, but now he is found." So the party began."*

(Luke 15:23-24)

In the story, Jesus is telling us that God is this good father. Just like a selfish son who disrespects his father, or a whoring wife who betrays her husband, we have abandoned God. And despite our rejection, he patiently waits for our return. When we come to him, he does not make us grovel for forgiveness but throws a massive party.

This is God.

God is a good dad. He is not like our imperfect earthly fathers and he will never wrong, mistreat or abandon you.

This is God's heart, and understanding this radical dimension of his love is the stepping-stone for what is to come.

Key Points:

- The angel tells Mary to name the child who is to be born to her *Jesus*, which means "God is salvation."
- God is a good dad who patently waits for us to come home.

EIGHT

BLOOD AND WATER

THE FIRST FOUR books in the New Testament are historical accounts of Jesus' life. We will be looking primarily at the book of John which was written by one of Jesus' closest disciples, John. At the start of this book, we are introduced to another John named John the Baptist.

> *"There was a man sent from God, whose name was John."*
>
> (John 1:6) [95]

In the book of Luke, the angel Gabriel comes to a priest named Zechariah and tells him that his wife will have a son they are to name John. Gabriel tells Zechariah that his son will "*prepare the people for the coming of the Lord.*"[96] John is the one chosen by God to prepare Israel for the Messiah.

The name that Zechariah is commanded to give his son is significant because John means "God is gracious."[97] John is called to prepare Israel to meet the Messiah by revealing the grace of God. The new covenant that the Messiah comes to initiate is a covenant of grace, a covenant not based on works, but freely given by God.[98]

Mikveh

John begins preaching in the wilderness of Judea and calling Israel to repent of their sins and prepare for the coming of the Messiah.[99] People from all around the region come to hear John's message and receive his baptism. The word "baptize" comes from the Greek word "baptizō" which can be translated:

I. to dip repeatedly, to immerse, to submerge (of vessels sunk)

II. to cleanse by dipping or submerging, to wash, to make clean with water, to wash one's self, bathe

III. to overwhelm[100]

This baptism John was engaging in was the well-known Jewish practice of mikveh, which is a ceremonial cleansing in water. Circumcision was a requirement for any male that wanted to become a Jew and all converts had to also go through a mikveh, which signified a washing away of former sins.[101] But John was baptizing *Jews* which caused confusion with the religious leaders who question his authority to alter their tradition.[102]

Why did John use mikveh (baptism) to prepare Israel for the coming of the Messiah? A person coming up from the mikveh was a picture of someone that had been cleansed of sin. What is interesting is that the Jewish Rabbis considered one who converts to Judaism after rising from the waters of mikveh to be like a "new born child."[103] One was also considered to go through this same kind of spiritual rebirth when married.[104] Today in Judaism, one of the main uses for mikveh is to prepare a bride before her wedding.[105] What this means is that John's baptism may have been, quite literally, a preparation for Israel to ready herself for the new marriage covenant the Messiah would introduce.[106]

Before a Jewish priest could come before God and offer sacrifices on behalf of the nation, he was required to do a mikveh.[107] Likewise, Israel was to prepare for the Messiah by repenting of sin and coming to him with a pure heart.[108]

In John 1:31, John the Baptist says,

> *"I have been baptizing with water so that he [Jesus] might be revealed to Israel."*[109]

Here John tells us that he was baptising to *reveal* the Messiah, and was another reason John used mikveh as a sign. As we will soon see, Jesus himself comes to John to be baptized, yet God does not need to be cleansed from sin because he is sinless. Why then does Jesus request this baptism? Perhaps we can find a clue in the strange name John gives Jesus upon seeing him.

> *"The next day John saw Jesus coming toward him and said, 'Look! The Lamb of God who takes away the sin of the world!'"*
>
> (John 1:29)

Calling Jesus the "Lamb of God who takes away the sin of the world" seems like a strange title, but the Jews would have known exactly what John was referring to. Each morning and evening in the temple, a pure lamb without physical defect was sacrificed.[110] For a Jew, the reference to a lamb would also bring to mind the Jewish feast of Passover which first took place in the book of Exodus.

In Exodus, God tells Moses that he is sending a final plague on Egypt where the angel of death will kill the first-born in every house across the land. After this plague, God says that Pharaoh will release the Israelites from slavery. He instructs Moses to tell the Israelites to sacrifice a lamb and smear its blood across their doorposts so that when the angel of death comes, he will see the blood and pass over their house.[111]

John also makes it clear that this is no ordinary lamb, but Jesus is the lamb who "takes away the sin of the world."[112] John is saying that Jesus will be a sacrifice made for the world's sin. And who is it that can offer a sacrifice before God?

A priest.

And how is a priest initiated into his office?

Through mikveh.[113]

Baptism was used to reveal Jesus the Messiah as Israel's High Priest, the only one who could enter the Holy of Holies in the temple and present sacrificial blood to cover the people's sins.

The Wedding Feast

In the next chapter of John we find Jesus attending a wedding in a small town called Cana.[114]

> *"On the third day there was a wedding at Cana in Galilee, and the mother of Jesus was there.* ***2*** *Jesus also was invited to the wedding with his disciples.* ***3*** *When the wine ran out, the mother of Jesus said to him, "They have no wine."* ***4*** *And Jesus said to her, "Woman, what does this have to do with me? My hour has not yet come."* ***5*** *His mother said to the servants, "Do whatever he tells you."* ***6*** *Now there were six stone water jars there for the Jewish rites of purification, each holding twenty or thirty gallons.* ***7*** *Jesus said to the servants, "Fill the jars with water." And they filled them up to the brim.* ***8*** *And he said to them, "Now draw some out and take it to the master of the feast." So they took it.* ***9*** *When the master of the feast tasted the water now become wine, and did not know where it came from (though the servants who had drawn the water knew), the master of the feast called the bridegroom* ***10*** *and said to him, "Everyone serves the good wine first, and when people have drunk freely, then the poor wine. But you have kept the good wine until now."* ***11*** *This, the first of his signs, Jesus did at Cana in Galilee, and manifested his glory. And his disciples believed in him."*
>
> (John 2:1-11)[115]

There are a few strange things in this text that we need to unpack to understand. Why does Mary ask Jesus to provide wine, and why does Jesus seem to refuse? What does he mean when he says, "My hour has not yet come"? To address Mary's request for Jesus to provide wine, we need to know a bit about ancient Jewish weddings.

Simply put, weddings were a *big* deal. The entire community was invited to the event which would last for days.[116] Wine was a key component of the feast and was supplied by the bridegroom.[117] To run out of wine during the wedding would have been a disaster because it was considered the most essential element to the party and would result in the humiliation of the newly married couple.[118]

With this in mind, it makes more sense why Mary insists Jesus do something miraculous to save the day.[119] But by requesting Jesus to miraculously provide wine for the wedding, she is asking him to step into the role of the bridegroom who was responsible for supplying the wine.[120] This may give us a clue as to why Jesus seems reluctant to fulfill her request. Jesus replies, "Woman, what does this have to do with me? My hour has not yet come." There are two things to note in this verse. First, to our ears it may sound like Jesus is being rude to his mother by addressing her as "woman", but culturally this is not the case.[121] Second, if we jump further ahead in the story, we discover that the term "my hour," that Jesus uses is a code that refers to his death.[122]

Okay, let's recap the situation. Mary asks Jesus to step into the role of the bridegroom and produce miraculous wine for the wedding. Jesus looks at her and essentially says, *What does this have to do with me? My time to die has not yet come.* Why does Jesus associate providing supernatural wine for a wedding with his death? Think back to the prophecy in Isaiah of the great banquet God will provide where it says,

> *"On this mountain the Lord Almighty will prepare a feast of rich food for all peoples, a banquet of aged wine—the best of meats and the finest of wines."*
>
> (Isaiah 25:6)[123]

This prophecy, which the Jews considered a picture of the messianic age, goes on to describe how God will swallow up death, wipe away the people's tears and remove their disgrace forever. But in order for God's wrath against evil to be satisfied there needs to be a sacrifice: a perfect sacrifice to atone for sin. Jesus knew that his mission was to be that sacrifice. It was his death that would bring about the wedding feast of the new covenant.

Still, what does wine have to do with Jesus' death? We are given another clue in verse six.

> *"Now there were six stone water jars there for the Jewish rites of purification, each holding twenty or thirty gallons. 7 Jesus said to the servants, "Fill the jars with water." And they filled them up to the brim."*
>
> (John 2:6-7)[124]

Together, these jars would have held between 120-180 gallons and were used for the "Jewish rites of purification." What is this a reference to?

Mikveh.[125]

Jesus takes the jars used for holding the ritual water that symbolised purification from sin and transforms its contents into wine that will save the wedding. The wine is representative of his blood. Just as a lamb's blood was used to purify Israel, Jesus' blood would be used to cleanse them from sin.

Not only does this type of blood bring joy and life to the party, it removes the otherwise inevitable shame of the bride and groom. By doing his first miracle at a wedding and stepping into the bridegroom's position, Jesus is making a statement. He is establishing himself as not only the Messiah, but as Israel's bridegroom.

Key Points:

- Mikveh, or baptism, was symbolic of one's repentance from sin and was used by John to prepare Israel for the coming of the Messiah.
- Jesus' baptism reveals his role as High Priest.
- John gives Jesus the title, "The Lamb of God who takes away the sin of the world."
- Jesus' first miracle revealing that he is the Messiah takes place at a wedding feast where he steps into the role of the bridegroom.

NINE

AN UNLIKELY INVITATION

AT THE WEDDING in Cana, Jesus performs his first miracle and begins to reveal his identity as Israel's bridegroom. In the following chapter we are taken to a scene with John the Baptist.

> *"So John's disciples came to him and said, "Rabbi, the man you met on the other side of the Jordan River, the one you identified as the Messiah, is also baptizing people. And everybody is going to him instead of coming to us."* ***27*** *John replied, "No one can receive anything unless God gives it from heaven.* ***28*** *You yourselves know how plainly I told you, 'I am not the Messiah. I am only here to prepare the way for him.'* ***29*** *It is the bridegroom who marries the bride, and the best man is simply glad to stand with him and hear his vows.*

> *Therefore, I am filled with joy at his success.* **30** *He must become greater and greater, and I must become less and less."'*
>
> (John 3:26-30)

Here John identifies Jesus as a *bridegroom* and himself as the *best man*. The English Standard Version of the Bible translates "best man" more literally in verse 29 as "friend of the bridegroom." The ancient Jews referred to the *friend of the bridegroom* as the "shoshabin." The closest modern comparison to the shoshabin would be a best man or maid of honour. Typically the bride and groom each had a shoshabin and although they were not always present in common weddings, they were never missing in marriages involving royalty.[126]

It was the shoshabin's role to glorify the bridegroom, not to take center stage at the wedding. This is why John does not complain about the attention shifting from his ministry to Jesus when he says, "He must become greater and greater, and I must become less and less."[127] John is saying that he has accomplished his goal of preparing Israel for her bridegroom and now he must allow the focus to shift to Jesus.

If there is still any doubt of Jesus' identity as bridegroom, they are put to rest when we learn that this is a title Jesus uses of himself in the other gospels.[128] But a question remains. If Jesus is the bridegroom, who is the bride? If God's plan is to institute a new marriage covenant with Israel and Jesus is the bridegroom, how is all this going to work? The next chapter of John drops some clues, but to set the scene let's briefly recap what has happened so far.

John's mission was to prepare Israel for her Messiah. He preached repentance from sin and used baptism as a physical representation of this cleansing. Given John's overt reference to Jesus as the bridegroom, it is possible that baptism was also given as a picture of the bride's preparation for her wedding.[129] In chapter two, Jesus attends a wedding where he steps into the role of bridegroom and produces supernatural wine. In the next chapter, John refers to Jesus as the bridegroom and himself as the best man. Now the scene is set for chapter four.

> *"Jesus knew the Pharisees had heard that he was baptizing and making more disciples than John* **2** *(though Jesus himself didn't baptize them—his disciples did).* **3** *So he left Judea and returned to Galilee.* **4** *He had to go through Samaria on the way."*
>
> (John 4:1-4)

The text mentions that Jesus had to go through Samaria. Many Jews despised the Samaritans so much that they would take a much longer journey around Samaria rather than walking through. The book of 2 Kings recounts how the Assyrian empire captured the land here known as Samaria and took thousands of Israelites into captivity.[130] The Assyrians then sent in their own colonists to populate the land as a way to decrease the chance of a rebellion.[131] This resulted in intermarrying between the Jews and the new peoples and a blending of Judaism with various pagan religions.

The Jews considered the Samaritan people an abomination because they had corrupted the religion and their bloodline.[132] The Samaritans were forbidden to worship at the temple in Jerusalem which led to the construction of a Samaritan temple on Mt. Gerizim.[133] In Jesus' time, a devout Jew would not talk or even associate with a Samaritan.[134] Jews wanted absolutely *nothing* to do with this disgraced people.

Returning to the story, we see Jesus do something out of the ordinary.

> *"Eventually he came to the Samaritan village of Sychar, near the field that Jacob gave to his son Joseph."* **5** *Jacob's well was there; and Jesus, tired from the long walk, sat wearily beside the well about noontime."*
>
> (John 4:5-6)

What is Jesus doing sitting beside a Samaritan well? The well was a convenient place for the single men to come to because they could interact with the women who came to draw water.[135] As a result, wells were a popular place for single men to come when looking to potentially marry a woman.[136] By stopping at a well, Jesus seems to be placing himself in a precarious position if you remember the six stage pattern we examined in the Old Testament where we saw three examples of men who came to wells in a foreign land. In each story, the man arriving at the well starts a chain of events that lead to a marriage.

Let's recap the stages:

A male foreigner arrives in a strange land.

He comes to a well.

A woman meets him at the well.

The woman runs home with a report.

The man is invited back to the woman's home.

This leads to an engagement or marriage.

By arriving in a Samaritan town and coming to a well, Jesus has already completed the first two stages. So far, Jesus looks like he could be a potential candidate for fulfilling this pattern. What is striking about the well Jesus comes to is that it is *Jacob's* well. This is the same Jacob who first met his wife Rachel at a well and whose name was later changed to "Israel" by God.[137] Jacob is the father of the nation Israel, the grandson of Abraham.

The plot thickens in the next verse.

> *"Soon a Samaritan woman came to draw water, and Jesus said to her, "Please give me a drink.""*
>
> (John 4:7)

A woman comes to the well. That's stage three. But what is even more shocking is Jesus' action when she comes to the well. He asks her for a drink! The fact that he talks to her, a despised Samaritan, should really get our attention.

The hour this woman comes to the well is also worthy of pointing out. It was around noon when this took place and the usual time for women to collect water was in the evening when it was cooler. It's as if this Samaritan woman is coming to the well at this odd hour because she does not want to be seen. Perhaps she was depressed, suffered from social anxiety or was afraid of meeting people from the community because she was considered an outcast.

When Jesus talks to her, the woman is clearly taken aback.

> *"The woman was surprised, for Jews refuse to have anything to do with Samaritans. She said to Jesus, "You are a Jew, and I am a Samaritan woman. Why are you asking me for a drink?"* ***10*** *Jesus replied, "If you only*

knew the gift God has for you and who you are speaking to, you would ask me, and I would give you living water."""

(John 4:9-10)

Speaking to the Samaritan, Jesus refers to this living water as "the gift God has for you". The Greek word translated "gift" implies that this living water is given freely with no strings attached.[138] One of the Jewish customs was if a man wanted to marry a woman he would offer her a gift called the *mohar* which can be translated as "bridal payment."[139] [140] The modern equivalent to this would be an engagement ring. We have seen an example of this before when Abraham's servant gives gifts to Rebekah after concluding she is God's chosen wife for Isaac.[141] There seems to be a connection with Jesus' offering of a gift with the wedding customs of the day, especially considering this conversation takes place at a well.

At first, the woman thinks the "living water" Jesus speaks of is physical.

""But sir, you don't have a rope or a bucket," she said, "and this well is very deep. Where would you get this living water? ***12*** *And besides, do you think you're greater than our ancestor Jacob, who gave us this well? How can you offer better water than he and his sons and his animals enjoyed?"* ***13*** *Jesus replied, "Anyone who drinks this water will soon become thirsty again.* ***14*** *But those who drink the water I give will never be thirsty again. It becomes a fresh, bubbling spring within them, giving them eternal life.""*

(John 4:14-14)

Here Jesus reveals that the gift he is offering her is eternal life.

> *""Please, sir," the woman said, "give me this water! Then I'll never be thirsty again, and I won't have to come here to get water."* ***16*** *"Go and get your husband," Jesus told her.* ***17*** *"I don't have a husband," the woman replied. Jesus said, "You're right! You don't have a husband—* ***18*** *for you have had five husbands, and you aren't even married to the man you're living with now. You certainly spoke the truth!""*
>
> (John 4:15-18)

Knowing the woman is not living in a proper relationship, he brings up her sin. He already knew about this but wants her to know that *he* knows too. His offer of living water is made with full knowledge of her current situation. Jesus isn't calling out her sin to shame her; he is showing his pursuit of her despite her sin.

> *""Sir," the woman said, "you must be a prophet.* ***20*** *So tell me, why is it that you Jews insist that Jerusalem is the only place of worship, while we Samaritans claim it is here at Mount Gerizim, where our ancestors worshiped?"* ***21*** *Jesus replied, "Believe me, dear woman, the time is coming when it will no longer matter whether you worship the Father on this mountain or in Jerusalem.* ***22*** *You Samaritans know very little about the one you worship, while we Jews know all about him, for salvation comes through the Jews.* ***23*** *But the time is coming—indeed it's here now—when true*

worshipers will worship the Father in spirit and in truth. The Father is looking for those who will worship him that way. ***24*** *For God is Spirit, so those who worship him must worship in spirit and in truth."* ***25*** *The woman said, "I know the Messiah is coming—the one who is called Christ. When he comes, he will explain everything to us."* ***26*** *Then Jesus told her, "I AM the Messiah!"* ***27*** *Just then his disciples came back. They were shocked to find him talking to a woman, but none of them had the nerve to ask, "What do you want with her?" or "Why are you talking to her?""*

(John 4:19-27)

After Jesus declares that he is the Messiah, his disciples arrive and are astonished to see what is taking place.

"The woman left her water jar beside the well and ran back to the village, telling everyone, ***29*** *"Come and see a man who told me everything I ever did! Could he possibly be the Messiah?"* ***30*** *So the people came streaming from the village to see him."*

(John 4:28-30)

The woman runs with a report. That's stage four.

"Many Samaritans from the village believed in Jesus because the woman had said, "He told me everything I ever did!" ***40*** *When they came out to see him, they*

*begged him to stay in their village. So he stayed for two days, **41** long enough for many more to hear his message and believe."*

(John 4:39-41)

Now the town invites Jesus to stay with them which completes stage five.

"Then they said to the woman, "Now we believe, not just because of what you told us, but because we have heard him ourselves. Now we know that he is indeed the Savior of the world.""

(John 4:42)

Then the scene ends.

But wait a minute. Where is the wedding? Jesus goes through the first five stages of the pattern and it seems like everything is pointing to an engagement or wedding, and it doesn't happen? But then again, maybe what we are looking for is hidden in plain sight.

God's plan is to bring about a new marriage covenant with Israel which means this covenant goes beyond just two people. We know Jesus completes stage five in verse 40 which leaves us with two verses for stage six to take place. Let's read those last verses again.

"When they came out to see him, they begged him to
*stay in their village. So he stayed for two days, **41** long*
enough for many more to hear his message and believe.
***42** Then they said to the woman, "Now we believe, not*

> *just because of what you told us, but because we have heard him ourselves. Now we know that he is indeed the Savior of the world.""*
>
> (John 4:40-42)

Rather than a physical marriage taking place, the citizens of the village come to faith in Jesus. There is an unstated parallel between marriage and belief.[142] A betrothal *does* take place in the scene; it's between Jesus and the entire town. Jesus is revealing that the new covenant is based on grace, not on obeying the law (Ten Commandments). The marriage of the new covenant is freely given by God and all it takes is faith to receive.

Still, why does Jesus come to a Samaritan woman to enact a symbolic betrothal between himself and the Samaritan people? This seems unexpected. The Samaritans were despised by the Jews and that the Messiah would establish the new covenant with them seemed unthinkable. As a prospective bride, the Samaritan woman has no business even being considered by Jesus. First off, she is a Samarian. That means there is no chance a respectable Jewish teacher would marry her. Then there's the fact that she has likely been divorced several times. Even if she was a Jew, this would make her a highly undesirable match for a rabbi.[143] To add to all this, we learn she is currently living in an improper relationship with a man. By Jewish standards this woman should be shunned and held in contempt, but this is the woman Jesus approaches.

I can just hear Jesus' heart call out as he sits with her. *I see you. I see your brokenness and your pain. I see how your heart has been ripped apart, piece by piece through your relationships. I see your stains. I know your heart.*

I know you have come to the well at this hour because you do not want anyone to see you. Even when you saw me sitting here, a feeling of dread descended over you because you believed I would see your sin and curse you. You were right about one thing. I do see your sin, but I have a plan to take care of that. You thought you were coming here to collect water, but I am here to give you something much more essential. I come to give you living water; water that will restore your heart and wash away your sin and shame forever. The truth is, there is nothing you can do to earn this gift, but I give it to you freely.

Your entire life you have been searching for love. Your entire life has been spent searching for me. And not once have I taken my eye off of you. That's right. I have always known you as mine, my beautiful one. And I am calling you to me.

I know you think that's impossible, but nothing is impossible with God. I have provided a sacrifice that will make the impossible possible. You know you have done nothing to deserve being worthy of my invitation to spend our lives together. And you're right. This is my gift of grace. I love you. I have always loved you and I am willing to die that I might be with you, my beloved one. Will you accept my gift? Will you say yes to me?

God gives the ultimate invitation to the least likely person. Tim Keller comments on the passage saying,

> "When Jesus was talking to the woman at the well… why when she asks for living water did he turn to her romantic life? Why when she said I want the water of life did he start talking about her sex life and her romances and about how she had always centred her life around men? You know what he is saying? You've been looking for the water of life in love. You've been

> looking for the water of life in romance. But unless you make me your one true love, you'll never find what you're looking for."[144]

Think back to the book of Hosea where the prophet is told to marry a prostitute who cheats on him to demonstrate what Israel has done to God. Despite Israel's betrayal, in chapter two God says that he will win her back and make her his "*wife forever*". At that time, the Jews were separated into two nations: Israel in the north and Judah in the south. The woman God addresses in Hosea chapter two is the northern kingdom of Israel. But in the time of Jesus, the northern kingdom no longer existed. What then was the name now given to the territory formerly known as the northern kingdom?

Samaria.[145]

Jesus symbolically betroths himself to the Samaritan woman and reveals that he has not given up on his rebellious first love. He will pursue her despite her sin, and win her back.

Key Points:

- John calls Jesus a "bridegroom."
- Jesus offers the Samaritan woman the gift of salvation.
- Jesus' interaction with the Samaritan does not end with a wedding, but with her town coming to belief in him.

TEN

THE BRIDE PRICE

IN JOHN 12, Jesus rides into Jerusalem on a donkey and presents himself as king to fulfil Zechariah 9:9 which the Jews believed referred to the Messiah.[146]

> *"Rejoice, O people of Zion! Shout in triumph, O people of Jerusalem! Look, your king is coming to you. He is righteous and victorious, yet he is humble, riding on a donkey—riding on a donkey's colt."*
>
> (Zechariah 9:9)

Shortly after this, Jesus preaches his last public sermon where he compares God's kingdom to a wedding feast.

> *"The Kingdom of Heaven can be illustrated by the story of a king who prepared a great wedding feast for his son."*
>
> (Matthew 22:2)

Then at the opening of John 13 we hear a familiar phrase.

> *"Before the Passover celebration, Jesus knew that his hour had come to leave this world and return to his Father."*
>
> (John 13:1)

Jesus referred to this "hour" while attending the wedding in Cana and is now revealing that his time to die has arrived.

Finally we arrive at the Last Supper where Jesus gathers with his disciples to celebrate Passover. Jewish families observed Passover by killing a perfect male lamb and eating it with unleavened bread to commemorate God's deliverance of Israel from slavery in Egypt.[147] While the family ate, the father would lead the household in explaining the meal's significance.[148] Yet when Jesus breaks the bread, he says something out of the ordinary.

> *"He took some bread and gave thanks to God for it. Then he broke it in pieces and gave it to the disciples, saying, "This is my body, which is given for you. Do this to remember me.""*
>
> (Luke 22: 19)

Jesus tells them that the Passover bread is his body. He is stating that the Passover meal actually points to him.

Unlocking the Mystery of the Grail

In the next verse, Jesus takes a cup that many have called the Holy Grail. Our journey through the Jewish scriptures and the life of Jesus now positions us to understand the significance of what Jesus was about to reveal.

> *"After supper he took another cup of wine and said, "This cup is the new covenant between God and his people—an agreement confirmed with my blood, which is poured out as a sacrifice for you.""*
>
> (Luke 22:20)

Here Jesus makes an astonishing revelation. Once again he changes the interpretation of the Passover meal and declares that he is initiating the new marriage covenant spoken of in Jeremiah 31.

> *""The day is coming," says the Lord, "when I will make a new covenant with the people of Israel and Judah.* ***32*** *This covenant will not be like the one I made with their ancestors when I took them by the hand and brought them out of the land of Egypt. They broke that covenant, though I loved them as a husband loves his wife," says the Lord.* ***33*** *"But this is the new covenant I will make with the people of Israel after those days," says the Lord. "I will put my instructions deep within them, and I will write them on their hearts. I will be their God, and they will be my people.* ***34*** *And they will not need to teach their neighbors, nor will they need to teach their relatives, saying, 'You should know the Lord.' For everyone, from the least to the greatest,*

> *will know me already," says the* L*ORD. "And I will forgive their wickedness, and I will never again remember their sins."'"*
>
> (Jeremiah 31:31-34)

The imagery Jesus uses in describing this new covenant would have shocked his disciples. Notice that Jesus compares the wine to his own blood. This would have been a stunning idea for a Jew to entertain because God had expressly told the Israelites not to drink blood.

> *"And if any native Israelite or foreigner living among you eats or drinks blood in any form, I will turn against that person and cut him off from the community of your people,* ***11*** *for the life of the body is in its blood. I have given you the blood on the altar to purify you, making you right with the* L*ORD. It is the blood, given in exchange for a life, that makes purification possible."*
>
> (Leviticus 17:10-11)[149]

We know the Jews took great offence to this reference of drinking blood because many of Jesus' followers abandoned him when he said it was necessary to eat his flesh and drink his blood to inherit eternal life.[150] Just as the blood of animals was used to atone for the Israelites sin, Jesus is saying that his blood "which is poured out as a sacrifice" will be used to purify them.[151]

To fully understand the symbolism of Jesus associating the Passover cup of wine with the new covenant of Jeremiah 31, we need to understand a bit about the Jewish wedding customs of the day. If a man wanted to marry a woman in ancient Israel, a bride price would have to be negotiated with her father. Once the wedding contract (ketubah) had been accepted by the woman's father, the prospective groom would offer the woman a cup of wine. If she declined to drink, she rejected his proposal. But if she drank, they were considered legally married.

If the woman accepted, the groom returned to his father's house to build an addition onto the home for his bride. The separation that lasted while the son built this house could last for over a year. Once the man's father had approved that the house was finished, the son would gather his friends and return to the woman's town, usually in the evening, and blast a ram's horn to announce that he had arrived for his bride. Throughout the separation, the bride did not know when the groom would return and she had to have her things packed and ready to leave at all times. At the groom's return, the marriage would finally be consummated and a massive wedding feast would take place.[152]

With this knowledge, another dimension is unlocked in Jesus' action. In declaring the cup of wine the new covenant in his blood, Jesus is engaging in what could have been understood as a marriage proposal.[153] [154] Here we begin to unlock the mystery of the Grail. In western culture, a man proposes by buying a ring and offering it to the woman he loves. In ancient Jewish culture, a man took a cup of wine and offered it to his beloved to seal the covenant.

The real treasure of the Grail is not the cup, but what it represents. The bride price Jesus offers is his life. Jesus is saying that *he* is the Passover lamb. Just as a lamb was killed in Egypt and its blood used to protect the Israelites from death, Jesus offers his life as a sacrifice to rescue Israel from sin and death. He comes to his bride and says, *I love you so much that I am willing to pay the highest price for you. I love you so much that I am will die so we can be together.*

Following their meal, Jesus continues to use marital language when speaking to his disciples.

> *""Don't let your hearts be troubled. Trust in God, and trust also in me.* ***2*** *There is more than enough room in my Father's home. If this were not so, would I have told you that I am going to prepare a place for you?* ***3*** *When everything is ready, I will come and get you, so that you will always be with me where I am.""*
>
> (John 14:1-3)

Jesus speaks of going to his father's home (heaven) to prepare a place for his followers. This is an unmistakable description of a Jewish bridegroom leaving to build a home for his bride.

Tragedy to Triumph

After the Passover meal we find Jesus in a garden praying in such agony that he begins to sweat drops of blood.[155] This condition is called hematidrosis which is triggered by a high degree of stress. Intense anxiety can cause certain chemicals to break down the capillaries in one's sweat glands and results in bleeding. The stress Jesus experiences here is unimaginable. He knows what is coming. Crucifixion was the worst possible way to die and was designed to inflict the maximum amount of pain for the longest duration of time. In fact, the agony from this death was so incredible that a new word was invented to describe the suffering on the cross: *excruciating*.

In the garden, Jesus is betrayed by one of his disciples and is captured by the Jewish religious leaders who bring him before the Roman governor Pilate where they demand his execution for claiming to be the Son of God. Pilate finds no fault in Jesus and tries to release him, but the religious leaders demand his death. Finally relenting, Pilate washes his hands and declares himself innocent of the sentence before handing Jesus over to be crucified. Pilate's action is significant because the Passover lamb had to undergo an intense inspection to ensure that it had no faults or blemishes. Once the one who had examined it was satisfied that it was without fault, he would wash his hands before handing the animal over to be sacrificed.[156]

After being severely whipped, Jesus is taken to a hill called Golgotha to be crucified. When we return to the prophecies made of the Messiah in the book of Isaiah, we see how Jesus' death specifically fulfilled them.

> *"Yet it was our weaknesses he carried; it was our sorrows that weighed him down. And we thought his troubles were a punishment from God, a punishment for his own sins!* **5** *But he was pierced for our rebellion, crushed for our sins. He was beaten so we could be whole. He was whipped so we could be healed.* **6** *All of us, like sheep, have strayed away. We have left God's paths to follow our own. Yet the* L*ORD* *laid on him the sins of us all."*
>
> (Isaiah 53:4-6)

As the crucifixion scene continues, we hear Jesus scream out a devastating cry.

> *"At about three o'clock, Jesus called out with a loud voice, "Eli, Eli, lema sabachthani?" which means "My God, my God, why have you abandoned me?""*
>
> (Matthew 27:46)

Just as the nation's sins were transferred to the sacrificial lamb, so too the sins of humanity were placed on Jesus.[157]

Shortly after this Jesus cried out, "It is finished" and dies. To ensure he was dead, a Roman soldier pierces Jesus' side.

> *"But one of the soldiers pierced his side with a spear, and at once there came out blood and water."*
>
> (John 19:34)[158] [159]

Following his death, Jesus is placed in a tomb near the crucifixion site. Three days later he rises from the dead and appears to hundreds of people before ascending into heaven.[160] Before he departs, Jesus tells his disciples to go into the entire world to baptize and spread the good news of his life and resurrection.

Jesus' death on the cross appears to be the ultimate tragedy. God comes to earth as a man who lives a perfect life and dies a torturous death. But Jesus' death is not a tragedy; it is God's crowning achievement. His sacrifice on the cross is the ultimate expression of love for humanity. Through his death, Jesus made it possible for mankind to be reconciled to God. As our high priest, Jesus comes before the Father and offers himself as a perfect sacrifice for the sins of the world. He paid our debt. Salvation is a gift from God and there is nothing we can add to it. All one has to do is turn from sin and place their faith in Jesus to be washed clean. This means you can stop beating yourself up for all your shortcomings and failures because Jesus already took your punishment. Before his death, Jesus tells his disciples that when he leaves he will send them the Holy Spirit which he calls "the Helper."

> *""Nevertheless, I tell you the truth: it is to your advantage that I go away, for if I do not go away, the Helper will not come to you. But if I go, I will send him to you.* ***8*** *And when he comes, he will convict the world concerning sin and righteousness and judgment.""*
>
> (John 16:7-8)[161]

Jesus promises to send the Holy Spirit who will live inside of his disciples.[162] There is an amazing truth here. God says the Spirit comes to convict the world of righteousness. When a person places their trust in Jesus, the Spirit dwells within them. But how can God live inside a sinful person? Here is the incredible reality. While a believer in Jesus is still a sinner, the Father's wrath is no longer against them. All his anger was placed on Jesus at the cross. When the Father looks at a believer, he sees Jesus: he sees perfection. When God looks at a disciple of Christ he doesn't see evil, filth or sin; he sees the righteousness of his Son who he loves perfectly! This is confirmed in a prayer Jesus prays to his Father for his Church.[163]

> *““I am in them and you are in me. May they experience such perfect unity that the world will know that you sent me and that you love them as much as you love me.””*
>
> (John 17:23)

God loves those who have put their faith in Jesus with the same love that God shares in the Trinity. Wow. This is God restoring the dance lost in the garden. Through Jesus, God is inviting humanity back into perfect relationship with him. God is turning the story that looked like an irreversible tragedy into something incredible.

Key Points:

- Jesus initiates the marriage of the new covenant with his 12 disciples through offering a cup of wine.
- The bride price Jesus offers is his life.
- Just as a Jewish bridegroom would return to his father's house and prepare a place for his bride, on the eve of his death, Jesus tells his disciples he is returning to his Father to prepare a place for them.
- By dying for the sins of the world and rising from the dead, Jesus is restoring mankind's relationship with God that was broken in the garden.

ELEVEN

THE UNVEILING

THE MOVIE *MAN OF STEEL* opens with a world in crisis. The core of planet Krypton has become unstable which threatens the Kryptonian people's survival. A man named Jor-El sends his only son to a distant planet called Earth before his world is destroyed. The boy is adopted by a couple in Kansas and given the name Clark Kent, but the world knows him as Superman. In the film, General Zod, a Kryptonian, arrives to earth and demands the world surrender Superman or face annihilation. Superman chooses to surrender himself to the US military and is given over to Zod. By the end of the film, Superman saves the world, defeats the enemy and rescues Lois Lane, a reporter at the Daily Planet with whom he is falling in love. Before surrendering to Zod, Superman has a chance to talk with Lois and she asks him what the "S" on his chest means. He replies by telling her that it is a symbol from his world that means *hope*.

We love superheroes because they touch the longings in our hearts. Superheroes fight battles and are caught up in great adventures; they give themselves to rescue and win the heart of a beautiful woman. Superheroes accomplish great things. Superheroes find love. Superheroes are beautiful. Superheroes give us hope.

In the film *Superman Returns*, Superman saves the world from destruction and dies from a wound in his side. All seems lost, but then, suddenly, he rises from the dead. He defeats the impossible and overcomes death.

One cannot help but see glimpses of Jesus here. Jesus is sent to earth by his Father where he saves the world, dies and defeats death by rising from the dead. Even in the original comic book series, Superman is killed and comes back to life. And then something happens that readers longed to see for decades. Finally, he marries Lois Lane.[164] The ultimate Superhero triumphs over death and marries the woman of his dreams.

Could it be that we are attracted to superheroes like Superman because the story of a hero giving himself out of love for the world and for a woman is the story God has been revealing throughout history? Could it be that our hearts jump when we hear Superman-like stories because they carry an echo of the ultimate story that God established before the foundation of the world? Could it be that God designed our hearts to long for someone beyond ourselves to rescue us and take us on a great adventure because it points to his future plan?

The Living One

In Genesis 17:19 God tells Abraham that his wife Sarah will have a son they are to call Isaac. This birth will be miraculous because Sarah is barren and beyond her childbearing years. Where have we heard of another miraculous birth?

Jesus.

In Genesis 22:2 God comes to Abraham and tells him to go to the land of Moriah and sacrifice his son on a mountain. In the New Testament we also see the Father offering up his Son.

> *"For this is how God loved the world: He gave his one and only Son, so that everyone who believes in him will not perish but have eternal life."*
>
> (John 3:16)

Once they reach the mountain, Isaac carries the wood for the burnt offering on his shoulders.

> *"And Abraham took the wood of the burnt offering and laid it on Isaac his son. And he took in his hand the fire and the knife. So they went both of them together."*
>
> (Genesis 22:6)[165]

Just as Isaac carried the wood for the sacrifice, Jesus carried the wood for the sacrifice.

> *"Carrying the cross by himself, he went to the place called Place of the Skull (in Hebrew, [Golgotha])."*
>
> (John 19:17)

Now we come to the only recorded conversation between Abraham and his son.

> *"And Isaac said to his father Abraham, "My father!" And he said, "Here I am, my son." He said, "Behold, the fire and the wood, but where is the lamb for a burnt offering?"* ***8*** *Abraham said, "God will provide for himself the lamb for a burnt offering, my son." So they went both of them together."*
>
> (Genesis 22:7-8)

Abraham says, "*God* will provide for himself the lamb for a burnt offering, *my son*." Later in the chapter we see that God *does* in fact provide an animal for the sacrifice, but it's a ram. Who is the true lamb God *himself* will provide? John the Baptist declares the answer.

> *"The next day John saw Jesus coming toward him and said, "Look! The Lamb of God who takes away the sin of the world!"*
>
> (John 1:29)

The Father would provide *himself*, the lamb for the offering: Jesus, his only Son.

> *"When they arrived at the place where God had told him to go, Abraham built an altar and arranged the wood on it. Then he tied his son, Isaac, and laid him on the altar on top of the wood."*
>
> (Genesis 22:9)

Recall that Isaac, a fully grown man, could have easily resisted being bound, but he submits to his father. It's the same with Jesus. As if the connection to Jesus in the story were not already strong enough, just before Abraham sacrifices his son, the angel of the LORD intervenes which many scholars believe *is* Jesus. Jesus shows up in the middle of this event as if to demonstrate how this act of a father offering his son is a prophetic sign that points to a future event where he will assume Isaac's role as the sacrifice. Only this time, the son will not be spared.

After Abraham sacrifices the ram in Isaac's place, he calls the mountain "the LORD will provide." It appears he chooses this name because God provides a sacrifice in Isaac's place, but there is a deeper significance here. There is a sense that in the future God *will* provide in this place again. Amazingly, it was on this same mountain that Jesus was crucified![166] [167]

Two-thousand years after Jesus intervened and stopped Abraham from sacrificing Isaac, the Father would send his Son to the same mountain to be offered as the bride price of the new covenant where God himself would make atonement for humanity's sin.

This future event is foreshadowed in the text when Abraham is the only one recorded returning from the mountain.

> *"So Abraham returned to his young men, and they arose and went together to Beersheba. And Abraham lived at Beersheba."*
>
> (Genesis 22:19)[168]

The verse reads as if Isaac had in fact been offered and Abraham returns alone.

Once we reach chapter 24, Abraham sends his chief servant to find a bride for his son. By backtracking to chapter 15 we learn that this servant's name is Eliezer which means "God of Help". So far in the story we have established that Abraham represents the Father, Isaac the Son, but who is the Spirit? In the book of John we saw Jesus give the Spirit a name.

> *""Nevertheless, I tell you the truth: it is to your advantage that I go away, for if I do not go away, the Helper will not come to you. But if I go, I will send him to you."""*
>
> (John 16:7)

Jesus calls the Spirit "the Helper" which is what Eliezer means (God of help). In Genesis 24, Abraham sends out Eliezer to find a bride for his son. Once Eliezer reaches a well outside the city with his 10 camels, he asks God for a sign. He essentially says, *I will ask a woman for a sip of water and instead she will offer to spend her evening hauling water from the well for my 10 camels. This will be the sign that this is the right woman for Isaac.*[169] This is an outrageous request. What does this request say about the kind of person Abraham's servant is looking for? He is looking for someone committed to radical self-giving love, the same kind of love shared within the Trinity.

When Rebekah comes to the well she offers to water the 10 camels and once she finishes, Eliezer presents her with gold jewelry. These gifts would have been a tremendous offering of appreciation for a few hours of work. Eliezer responds to Rebekah's radical outpouring of love by lavishing on her what was exponentially more valuable than her gift of watering the camels.[170]

Rebekah is symbolic of Jesus' Church. Just as those who believe in Jesus agree to be united with one they have never seen, Rebekah agrees to go with Abraham's servant to marry a man she has never seen.

Finally, Isaac appears in the story for the first time since being offered on the mountain by Abraham.[171] He is united with Rebekah after coming from "the well of the Living One who sees me," the well dedicated to Jesus by Hagar. This is also the well where Jesus makes his first appearance in the Bible. In the next chapter we learn that Isaac and Rebekah move near this well to live.[172] Do you see why this is significant? Isaac meets his bride after coming from the location of Jesus' first appearance in scripture, a well dedicated to the Son. He then brings Rebekah back to the land with this well. This is a picture of Jesus being united with his bride.[173] And whose well does he lead her to? The well of the *Living One.* He is no longer dead, but alive!

The parallels between Isaac and Jesus are beyond coincidence. What is particularly incredible is the fact that Isaac's story took place nearly 2000 years before Jesus' birth. Long before Jesus arrived to earth as a man, God's plan was set.

But what if there were another story, one that carried clues of Jesus life and God's plan that took place 2000 years *before* Isaac. As we will see, from the very foundation of the world, God's plan has always been to prepare a bride for his son.

The Last Adam

Two-thousand years before Isaac, God created Adam.[174] The Bible tells us that Adam represents Jesus who is called "the last Adam."[175] The book of Romans says,

> *"Now Adam is a symbol, a representation of Christ, who was yet to come."*
>
> (Romans 5:14b)

In Genesis, God causes Adam to fall into a deep sleep where he takes one of Adam's ribs to make Eve.[176] Recall that the Hebrew word translated "ribs" is the same word more commonly translated as "side." In other words, Adam fell into a deep sleep and his side was pierced which brought forth his bride. Likewise, Jesus fell into the deep sleep of death on the cross and his side was also pierced, and it is through Jesus' death that brings about the salvation of his bride.

When Eve takes from the tree of the knowledge of good and evil, she offers the fruit to Adam. He knew that eating the fruit would result in death, but he follows her anyway. I think there is a spiritual foreshadowing taking place here. In a sense, Adam is showing Eve that he is willing to give his life so that he can be with her.[177] In the same way, Jesus willingly embraces death to be with his bride. He comes to earth and says *I'm willing to give up the glory of heaven, die the worst death and take all your sin upon myself so that we can be together.*

Think back to Isaac and Rebekah who are a picture of Jesus and the Church. One translation of Rebekah's name is "captivating." Adam was captivated by Eve's beauty, and, likewise, when Jesus looks upon his Church, he too is captivated.

The Father didn't create a partner that would not be to his Son's liking.

Isaac's name means "laughter." When I think of his name I am carried back to Jesus' first miracle at the wedding in Cana. What is Jesus' first sign to reveal himself as Israel's bridegroom? He creates tons of amazing wine to sustain the party and keep the laughter going. The wine is symbolic of his plentiful blood which is poured out to redeem the world from sin. I believe there is an echo in Isaac's name that carries over to what Jesus accomplished. Jesus' sacrifice is so amazing that our natural response should be laughter, joy and praise.

The ultimate tragedy of sin entering the world is redeemed by Jesus on the cross where he allows man's sin to magnify his love and grace. This was God's plan from the beginning. His plan has always been to turn the worst tragedy into his ultimate triumph. The story of mankind has always been about preparing a bride for the Son. It has always been a romance. All we need to do to confirm this is read the end of the story.

The Return to Eden

The last book in the Bible is called "Revelation" which can be translated as the "unveiling."[178] In this book, God pulls back the curtain and displays his plan for the world. Revelation is written by Jesus' disciple John and is the account of a vision he receives. Near the end of the book, the vision begins to intensify as the angel progresses to the climax of God's plan.

> *"Then I heard again what sounded like the shout of a vast crowd or the roar of mighty ocean waves or the crash of loud thunder: "Praise the LORD! For the Lord*

our God the Almighty, reigns. ***7*** *Let us be glad and rejoice, and let us give honor to him. For the time has come for the wedding feast of the Lamb, and his bride has prepared herself.* ***8*** *She has been given the finest of pure white linen to wear." For the fine linen represents the good deeds of God's holy people.* ***9*** *And the angel said to me, "Write this: Blessed are those who are invited to the wedding feast of the Lamb." And he added, "These are true words that come from God."*
10 *Then I fell down at his feet to worship him, but he said, "No, don't worship me. I am a servant of God, just like you and your brothers and sisters who testify about their faith in Jesus. Worship only God.""*

(Revelation 19:6-10a)

Whatever John saw and experienced, a glimpse of it caused him to begin worshiping the angel delivering the message.

We pick up the vision in chapter 21.

"I heard a loud shout from the throne, saying, "Look, God's home is now among his people! He will live with them, and they will be his people. God himself will be with them. ***4*** *He will wipe every tear from their eyes, and there will be no more death or sorrow or crying or pain. All these things are gone forever.""*

(Revelation 21:3-4)

Any knowledgeable Jew reading this passage would have seen how these words are strikingly familiar to how the prophet Isaiah describes the banquet God would throw during the Messiah's rule on earth,

> *"...he will swallow up death forever. The Sovereign LORD will wipe away the tears from all faces; he will remove his people's disgrace from all the earth. The LORD has spoken."*
>
> (Isaiah 25:8)[179]

Finally we reach the last chapter in the Bible: Revelation 22. It begins with a description of the new Eden.

> *"Then the angel showed me the river of the water of life, bright as crystal, flowing from the throne of God and of the Lamb* **2** *through the middle of the street of the city; also, on either side of the river, the tree of life with its twelve kinds of fruit, yielding its fruit each month. The leaves of the tree were for the healing of the nations."*
>
> (Revelation 22:1-2)[180]

Humanity's story begins in a garden with a wedding and it will end in a garden with a wedding. After seeing these things, John falls down and worships the angel again![181] John knew that he wasn't supposed to worship angels, but the weight and splendor of God's plan is so intense that his automatic response is to bow in praise.

The first human words recorded in the Bible are in the love song Adam sings upon seeing his bride.[182] In Revelation, we find the Bible closes in a harmony the Church sings with the Spirit. It is a song of the bride's longing for her husband.

> *"The Spirit and the bride say, "Come!"...Amen. Come, Lord Jesus."*
>
> (Revelation 22:17, 20b)

This is how the Bible ends. The bride, filled with the Spirit, calls out for her bridegroom.[183]

From cover to cover, the Bible is a love story. Two-thousand years after Jesus' life on earth, God's story continues. You are a character in this story, and God has not called you to play an insignificant role on the sidelines. God is inviting you to join him at the very heart of the adventure. He's inviting you to be his bride.

Key Points:

- The Bible begins and ends in a garden with a love song and a wedding. All of human history is leading up to the great wedding in Revelation where Jesus will be united with his Church.

TWELVE

BOY + GIRL = DIVINE PLAN

RECENTLY I SAT on the couch in my basement with my sister and cousin visiting from Sweden, looking for something to watch on Netflix. When we came across *Braveheart*, my cousin's voice jumped in excitement. "Yes! Let's watch *Braveheart*!" I was game, and the fact that my sister hadn't seen it made my cousin even more adamant that we had to see it.

The film opens in 13th century Scotland where William Wallace's people live in servitude to the English. Wallace marries his childhood sweetheart Murron in secret because the English ruler of the region rapes Scottish brides on their wedding day. One day an English soldier attacks Murron and tries to rape her in the town. Wallace comes to the rescue and throws off the men attacking his wife and tries to get her out of the village as quickly as possible. As she is riding away, a soldier hits her across the face with his spear and throws her to the ground. The commander of the town then executes her for resisting the rape.

Shortly after, Wallace returns to the town with his hands raised, pretending to surrender. When two guards approach him, Wallace pulls out a nunchaku and smashes the head of one of the men and stabs the other in the throat. A soldier that charges him loses a leg and the next is thrown down by Wallace's sword. Soon Scotsmen begin pouring into the streets and attacking the guards. Once the town is retaken, Wallace approaches the commander who murdered his wife and slits his throat. Word spreads of Wallace's courage and thousands of countrymen rally to him to begin a rebellion.

As the film progresses, Wallace leads his men to victory against the English but he is betrayed to the enemy and sentenced to a torturous death. After suffering terribly at his execution, Wallace is placed on a cross where he is disemboweled. As his organs are being ripped from him, the King's representative whispers in his ear, tempting him to say "mercy" and receive a quick death. In defiance, Wallace yells in a loud voice that fills the courtyard, "Freedom!"

As the executioner prepares the axe for the beheading, Wallace turns his head to the side, exhausted, and looks into the sea of people watching. He takes one last look at his two friends, concealed in the crowd, who have risked their lives coming to see him off. The three of them had fought bravely together. Then, suddenly, he sees a woman appear from behind them.

It's Murron.

She steps to the side of his friends and they lock eyes. She smiles. As the axe comes down on him, Wallace also manages a smile as he looks out at her.

In the final scene we see the Scots and English return to the battlefield. The Scottish king addresses his men and they scream out a cry and charge the enemy. Then we hear Wallace's voice one last time. As he narrates, he tells us that his countrymen fought, starving and outnumbered, at the fields of Bannockburn, and won their freedom.

By the time we finished the movie three-hours later, it was well after midnight. Although I was tired, I was also pumped and inspired. The next month, my sister was visiting for the weekend and wanted to watch a movie, so back we went to Netflix. When I scrolled passed *13 Going on 30*, my sister made it clear that she really wanted to see it. So we did.

The story revolves around 13-year-old Jenna Rink, a geeky girl who longs to be admired by the cool girls at school known as the Six Chicks. She dreams of growing up and becoming a beautiful woman successful in a career. On her birthday, Jenna's best-friend Matty gives her an elaborate, pink, dream doll house that he spent several weeks building. Inside the doll house, Jenna finds cut-outs of him and her inside. When the Six Chicks arrive at the party, Jenna, embarrassed of the dollhouse, hides it in her basement closet. There she closes her eyes and wishes that she could become 30.

When she opens her eyes, Jenna finds herself in a strange apartment and in her 30 year-old body. She quickly learns that she has become very successful working a job in New York at her favourite magazine while dating a famous hockey player on the New York Rangers. Yet despite her career success, Jenna discovers that she has become a very mean, selfish and demanding person. She tracks down Matty and is surprised to see that he has slimmed out and is very attractive.

He tells her that she became one of the Six Chicks in high school and stopped talking to him. Jenna tries to repair her friendship with Matty but a romance between them is suppressed because Matt is engaged.

On Matty's wedding day, Jenna rushes to his house and tells him that she is the one he should marry. Matty confesses that he has always loved her, but it's too late. He walks into his closet and pulls out the dream house he built for her years ago. Jenna asks for it and he gives it to her. Outside, she examines the house and cries. Then, she closes her eyes and is miraculously returned to her closet in her 13-year-old body. She rushes out and kisses Matty, realising that the person she longed to be with had been in front of her all along. In the next scene we see Jenna and Matty grownup, at their wedding. Then, just before the credits roll, we see the house that they are moving into. It's a life-sized version of the pink dream house he had built for her.

God and Gender

One way to find hints of the deep longings within men and women is to examine the movies they enjoy. My cousin was excited to watch *Braveheart* and my sister *13 gong on 30*. I enjoyed both of these movies, but why is it that we don't often see groups of men gathering to see romantic comedies and groups of women going out to see movies that focus on blood-soaked battles? It is because men and women are different.

I remember growing up wondering why men and women were different. What was God's reason for creating gender? Why not one gender? Why not three? God is a master designer and everything he creates has meaning. The Bible says that men and women are both created in God's image. This means that each gender reveals something distinct about him. By seeking to understand the uniqueness of each gender, we are seeking to understand God.

What are a couple of themes that run deep in a man's heart?

Men long to be the hero. In the heart of each man is a desire to fight and sacrifice himself for a great cause. For Wallace the cause was freeing his nation. For Matty, it was winning Jenna's love. Men often place their identity in their accomplishments and orient their lives around doing things to build their resumes to prove to the world and themselves that they are important and needed. Each man wants to know if he has what it takes to succeed. Each man wants to be seen as the hero. A man's desire to prove himself is so strong that it is often a major source of insecurity.

What does this desire tell us about God? It tells us that God has a warrior's heart. He does not need our love to boost his ego because he is perfectly secure in himself, but he longs for us to come to him because he is the ultimate source of love and joy. Each step we take towards him is a step closer to our happiness.

Men long to pursue and win the heart of a beautiful woman. Beauty captures a man's heart and inspires him to take action. It was Murron's death that galvanized Wallace to fight for his country and Jenna's beauty that inspired Matt to win her heart. A man's heart longs to delight a woman and bring her joy. He will go to the ends of the earth to win a woman he loves.

Likewise, God pursues us with the heart of a passionate

lover. When Jesus looks on his Church, his heart is filled with excitement. God went to his death to demonstrate his unending love for his bride. As a man's heart is captivated by a beautiful woman, God's heart is captivated by his Church.

What about women?

Women long to unveil beauty. There is a reason there are more clothing and cosmetic stores devoted to women. It has been estimated that in the United Kingdom, the average woman may spend £140,000 on hair and cosmetics in her lifetime.[184] We all know men's eyes are drawn to women, but research has also shown that women spend more time examining each other than they do men.[185] There is a mysterious beauty about the female body that fascinates both sexes. This longing to unveil beauty was one of the main reasons Jenna wanted to be validated by the popular girls at school and grow up to be a woman so quickly. The desire for beauty is so strong, and heightened by our ridiculous photoshopped standards, that image is a huge source of insecurity for both sexes, but especially women.

God created women to reveal his splendor. David was Israel's greatest king and wrote in the book of Psalms,

> *"One thing I ask from the LORD, this only do I seek: that I may dwell in the house of the LORD all the days of my life, to gaze on the beauty of the LORD and to seek him in his temple."*
>
> (Psalms 27:4)[186]

David's one desire was to gaze upon God's beauty, and God calls David "a man after his own heart."[187] God created women with a longing to unveil beauty because he longs to unveil beauty. In the same way a woman's beauty captures a man's heart, God longs for mankind to be captivated by his glory.

Women long to be pursued. We see this theme played out in the timeless Disney classics *Snow White*, *Sleeping Beauty* and *Cinderella*. It's not that a woman is helpless and in need of rescuing, it's that she desires to be seen for who she really is: a beautiful, unique person worthy of a prince's undying devotion. Mandy Hale, author of *The Single Woman* writes, "In my humble opinion…it's not a big mystery. We want to be pursued."[188] Staff at the popular dating site eHarmony state that women "long to feel cherished, pursued, and known."[189] God also wants you to pursue him. When you see God for who he is and realize the lengths he has gone so that you can encounter his beauty, you will be ever fascinated with his love and caught up in the adventure you were made for.[190]

The Mystery of Marriage

While men and women are different, we complement each other. This is obvious even in our bodies because they *literally* fit together. Yet when it comes to sex, God says that it is only for marriage. Why this restriction?

There are many practical reasons for not having sex outside of marriage. If you are interested in learning more about this I would encourage you to check out the chapter "Love, Sex and Dating" in the book *Thrive: A Guide for Life's Journey* that I co-authored with my friend Randy Conklin. But in the big picture, why does God restrict sex to marriage? To answer this question we need to understand the purpose of marriage.

Most people in Western culture believe marriage is about

self-fulfillment. People marry because they have faith the other person will make their life better. Here's the problem when two people enter a marriage with this mindset.

Marriage is not designed to be about you.

In the second chapter we saw how marriage was created to reflect the Trinity. Marriage is about displaying God and his selfless love. Just for the record, we fail horribly at this. The reason divorce rates have blown out of control over the last few decades is that we have been going about marriage wrong. God designed marriage to be about service and sacrifice. Marriage *is* about love, but we have been operating under a corrupt definition. Love is not feeling infatuated, it is choosing the highest good for the other person. Choosing the highest good for someone else usually has a cost and it's not always pleasant. There was a cost for God to rescue us from sin, but he paid the price *because* of love.

Marriage is designed to be most fulfilling and glorious when both partners orient their lives around serving the other. Can you imagine the beauty of a marriage where this selfless dynamic takes place? We all want to be served unconditionally, but we struggle to give because our hearts have been corrupted by sin. Yet God had a plan to restore our hearts which he reveals in Deuteronomy.

> *"And the Lord your God will circumcise your heart and the heart of your offspring, so that you will love the Lord your God with all your heart and with all your soul, that you may live."*
>
> (Deuteronomy 30:6)[191]

In Ezekiel God says,

> *"And I will give you a new heart, and I will put a new spirit in you. I will take out your stony, stubborn heart and give you a tender, responsive heart."*
>
> (Ezekiel 36:26)

When God's Spirit enters a believer they are given a new heart with new desires. This does not mean that a person will suddenly stop sinning, but that their heart will begin craving what is pleasing to God.[192] When God's Spirit enters a person, he gives them the power to make marriage successful. If marriage is modeled after God, it's going to take God for it to truly thrive. I'm not talking about having a nice functional marriage that doesn't end in divorce, but a passionate, awe-inspiring marriage where both lovers pour themselves out for each other and experience the sacrifice and joy of living in the shadow of the Trinity. No human marriage will be perfect, or even close to perfect, but God can empower you to live out marriage in the spirit of his design which is to reflect his love and display his glorious plan to the world.

How does a Spirit-led marriage display God's plan? While marriage is a reflection of the Trinity, it also points to something else. There is another dimension to marriage that reveals something stunning about God's desire and plan for those he loves. God unveils this understanding of marriage in the New Testament through a man named Paul in the book of Ephesians.

> *"As the Scriptures say, "A man leaves his father and mother and is joined to his wife, and the two are united into one." **32** This is a great mystery, but it is an illustration of the way Christ and the church are one."*
>
> (Ephesians 5:31-32)

Paul begins by referencing the first marriage between Adam and Eve.

> *"This explains why a man leaves his father and mother and is joined to his wife, and the two are united into one."*
>
> (Genesis 2:24)

He then explains how marriage is a picture of Jesus and his Church. From the very start, marriage has always modeled this reality. In a sense, marriage is a kind of play or performance. Within this covenant, the man is cast in the role of Jesus and the woman as the Church. The husband is to love and care for his wife as Jesus loves his Church, willing to give his life for her. In turn, the wife is to respect and honour her husband as the Church is to glorify God.[193] When husband and wife embrace these roles, marriage becomes a living picture of God's plan for the world. Commenting on this passage, Denny Burk says,

> "Adam and Eve's marriage (and every other marriage after it) is meant by God to be an icon of another marriage: Jesus' marriage to his bride, the church. So marriage is fundamentally about the glory of God,

> because it's meant to depict the gospel. It tells a bigger story: husbands loving their wives as Christ loved the church, and wives relating to their husbands as the church relates to Christ."[194]

When seen in this light, the splendor and power of what marriage represents becomes incredible. Marriage is so much more than falling in love and living life with someone for a few decades. Marriage is about displaying God's infinite plan to be united with his bride and cherish her forever. This truly is a great mystery!

In summary, marriage was designed to reveal two dimensions. The first is to give us a picture of the Trinity: lovers who become one and serve each other in perfect unity. The second is to unveil God's eternal plan for humanity: the preparation of a bride for the Son. Marriage points to the wedding feast in Revelation where the bride partners in life with Jesus and receives and gives his self-sacrificial love forever. Human marriage, then, is meant to display the love within the Trinity and reveal God's eternal plan for the world; a relationship beyond our wildest dreams; a marriage where the bride and groom live happily ever after. Ultimately, marriage is about giving God glory. It's not about you or even the one you married. It's about God.

The Mystery of Sex

Now that we have an idea of God's intention for marriage, we are better positioned to understand his plan for sex. Earlier we asked why God would restrict sex within marriage. The real question most people are asking is, "Why does God want to limit my fun and freedom?" Perhaps the deeper question that is implied is, "Why isn't God good?"

First, we know God is good which means his standards are designed for our benefit. Like any good father, God gives rules because he loves us and wants our best. One reason he tells us that sex is only to be shared between married couples is because he wants us to experience the maximum amount of pleasure. Research is now showing how married people have the most sex and the best sex and how sexual encounters outside marriage come with a variety of negative physical and emotional consequences.[195]

Still, there is a strong desire to pursue sex regardless of whether or not it's in marriage. We are faced with the same choice presented to Eve. It looks pleasant and appears so innocent. Do we trust that God is good or do we eat from the tree?

Our culture preaches that sex and marriage can be separated. But there is something very important we need to understand. God places marriage and sex in *one* category. He created them and said the two go together. If marriage is about glorifying God, *sex* is about glorifying God. If marriage is sacred, sex is sacred. If marriage is an act of worship, sex is an act of worship. Sex is not about seeking one's own pleasure at the expense of another, which so often is portrayed in pornography. This is the exact opposite of God's design.

Glenn Stanton writes, "Only the sexual embrace within marriage mirrors the nature of the Trinitarian relationship in creation. In the ideal, it's loving, permanent, exclusive, and self-giving. Premarital and extramarital sex can't mirror this reality."[196] In their book *The Meaning of Marriage,* Tim and Kathy Keller state, "Sex is for fully committed relationships because it is a foretaste of the joy that comes from being in complete union with God through Christ."[197] "In so many cases, when one person says to another, 'I love you, but let's not ruin it by getting married,' that person really means, 'I don't love you *enough* to close off all my options. I don't love you enough to give myself to you that thoroughly.'"[198]

God says sex is only for two people that have radically committed themselves to a permanent relationship of self-sacrificial love. Sex is a great joy designed for those that have merged themselves as one in every possible way: socially, economically and spiritually. It is only when two people have committed to a relationship in the likeness of the Trinity that sex can be expressed in its God-given context as an act of worship to glorify God.

God created sex for procreation, pleasure and to give us a peek into the joy he shares within himself. In addition, sex gives us a glimpse into the glory of God's future plan. Rob Jackson writes,

> "The physical union of our bodies was planned to be a picture of the joy we will have when finally joined with Christ at his return, our spiritual marriage. This is not to say our union with Christ will be sexual, but that our earthly expressions of sexuality in marriage are the closest approximation to the unity, joy, and pleasurable fulfillment we will experience in heaven."[199]

Sex is a glimpse into the pleasure believers will experience when they are united with God in heaven. It is a foreshadowing of the incredible intimacy that will belong to the Church when she sees Jesus face to face. It will not be a sexual experience, but something much greater; something so powerful and exciting that only sexual language is capable of giving a hint of this joy. John Piper says,

> God created us in his image, male and female, with personhood and sexual passions so that when he comes to us in this world there would be these powerful words and images to describe the promises and the pleasures of our covenant relationship with him through Christ. God made us powerfully sexual so that he would be more deeply knowable. We were given the power to know each other sexually so that we might have some hint of what it will be like to know Christ supremely.[200]

Describing how sex points to the glory of paradise, Peter Kreeft writes, "Sex…gives us subjectively a foretaste of heaven, of the self-forgetting, self-transcending self-giving that is what our deepest hearts are designed for, long for and will not be satisfied until they have, because we are made in God's own image and this self-giving constitutes the inner life of the Trinity."[201]

The Kellers write, "Sex is glorious not only because it reflects the joy of the Trinity but also because it points to the eternal delight of the soul that we will have in heaven, in our loving relationships with God and one another."[202] If all of this is true about sex pointing to heaven, then it's going to be a lot better than any images you have seen of people lazily playing harps in the clouds while eating cream cheese. The joy that awaits those God is preparing a place for is so stunning that it defies imagination.

The Future of Marriage

Until recently, one of Jesus' teachings on marriage seemed strange and disappointing to me.

> *""For when the dead rise, they will neither marry nor be given in marriage. In this respect they will be like the angels in heaven."""*
>
> (Matthew 22:30)

Jesus unequivocally states that earthy marriage will pass away in the resurrection. This was a verse I wished wasn't in the Bible because marriage and sex seemed like such an exciting part of life. Why would Jesus say that human marriage, something so beautiful, would pass away?

Imagine an orphanage filled with hundreds of children in a remote village. Most of the kids have spent their entire lives in this place and know nothing else. Each day a simple meal of bread and vegetables is served. However, on Fridays there is an exception. This day the children are each given a toothpick with a tiny sliver of dry meat. As the days pass, the children wait for this event with anticipation because the small piece of meat they receive is the most enjoyable food they experience.

One day a man travels to this distant orphanage to adopt a child. Once all the papers are finalized, the father is introduced to his child for the first time. He takes the child into his car and they begin the long journey home. The child, who has never sat in a car before, looks out the window intently, wondering what their home will be like. Turning to the father the child asks, "Will there be any toothpicks with pieces of meat where we are going?"

The father turns with a smile and says, "No, there won't be any toothpicks at our meals." The child's first reaction is dread because of the belief that there will only be bread and vegetables where they are going.

Upon arriving at their new home, the child is ushered into a great mansion. After meeting the new family, the father brings the child through two large oak doors to a banqueting hall. In front of them stands a table full of the best meats. There are trays overflowing with T-bone steaks, racks of ribs, lamb chops and other foods the child has never known. The child's mouth drops while looking at this exquisite display. The father bends down on his knee and points to the massive table in front of them and says, "You see that? It's all for you."

When the father said that there wouldn't be toothpicks with meat at his new home, the child concluded they were going to a place without meat. In truth, there was no need for toothpicks because of the abundance of meat. No longer was he confined to a morsel of meat once a week; now he was free to eat the finest foods every day for the rest of his life.

When we hear Jesus' words that human marriage is passing away, it is easy to react like the child and picture heaven as a place where marriage will be gone forever. Yet this is not what the Bible teaches. In heaven, human marriage will be dissolved because we will experience the marriage which it has pointed to all along. On this John Piper writes, "[H]uman marriage is temporary. To be sure, it points to something eternal, namely, Christ and the Church. But when this age is over, it will vanish into the superior reality to which it points."[203] Reverting to human marriage in heaven would be like craving toothpicks with tiny pieces of meat when a buffet of the best steaks stands before you.

Randy Alcorn says, "The Bible does not teach there is no marriage in heaven. The Bible teaches there is one marriage in heaven. Christ married to his bride, the Church."[204] When Jesus speaks of heaven saying "they will neither marry nor be given in marriage," he is describing how *human* marriage will pass away. Marriage and sexuality are signs that point to God's future plan. The little slices of meat we have grown to love on earth will be replaced by a feast so amazing that we will never desire to return to them.

Christopher West writes, "Our world worships the body, worships sex. Why? Because so many of us have come to believe that sexual union will satisfy our deepest hunger. The world is on to something here. For marital union is meant to be an icon of our ultimate satisfaction. It's meant to point us to Christ."[205] Love, romance, marriage and sexuality all come from God. He created us with these desires to reveal himself and his plan. Is it any wonder why our culture worships here? Our hearts are wired to crave these things because they point to God. Our world is worshiping at the sampler booths at Costco when God is offering everything stocked on the shelves. Love, sex, romance and marriage were never meant to be ends in themselves here on earth; they are signposts pointing to God and his plan of redemption.

Key Points:

- Men long to be the hero and win the heart of a beautiful woman. Women long to unveil beauty and be pursued. Through these desires, God is revealing his heart.
- Not only is marriage a reflection of the Trinity, it is a picture of God's plan for humanity. All of human history is leading to the marriage between Jesus and his Church.
- Human marriage and sexuality were designed to give us hints of the joy of relationship with God in heaven.
- In heaven, human marriage will pass away because we will have reached the greater reality that it has pointed to all along.

THIRTEEN

LOVE STORY

DECEMBER 19TH 2013,

It happened in an instant. Like a flash of light in my mind, it suddenly clicked. I couldn't help but laugh. *Really*? I focused my gaze on her again. *How had I not seen this before*? I was overcome. It finally made sense.

* * *

Do you remember how it first felt when you fell in love? The thrill of love can cause us to do radical things. By the time my dad was 19 he knew he wanted my mom. He showed up at her door with flowers.

She rejected him.

This was a problem because he was completely taken by her, so he did what any reasonable guy entranced by a woman does. He purchased her engagement ring. One day he asked if he could look at her nursing ring. It fit around his pinky finger so he had an idea of the size he needed to buy. While in Sweden, he went into a jewelry store and spent most of his savings on the ring. All this for a girl that had turned him down that he wasn't even dating! Thankfully my dad's crazy antics pulled through and I live to tell the tale.

When we are caught in love's grip, it's as if a magnetic force is drawing us to the other person. This unseen power that grips our heart stirs a desire to be united with this mysterious creature that looks similar to us, yet is different.

Understanding the Bride

We all come into this world built to give and receive love. Could it be that the desire in each of us to be united with another human being in love is part of a larger story written on our hearts? I believe this is the story God predestined for us before the dawn of time. Love is more than biology; it is a reflection of the heart of God. The Bible begins and ends with a wedding because the story God is telling throughout human history is about love.

There is a force that brings men and women together which is God's design. When a man and woman are joined in marriage they are acting out God's eternal plan. As we saw in the previous chapter, each gender has the privilege of displaying a specific role within marriage. The woman represents the Church and the man represents Jesus. A man is called to reveal God's sacrificial, passionate pursuit of humanity, and a woman is called to unveil the Church's joyful response.

We also discussed how marriage is a picture of the Trinity. The Kellers write,

> "Both women and men get to "play the Jesus role" in marriage – Jesus in his sacrificial authority, Jesus in his sacrificial submission. By accepting our gender

> roles, and operating within them, we are able to demonstrate to the world concepts that are so counterintuitive as to be completely unintelligible unless they are lived out by men and women in Christian marriages."[206]

The husband is called to sacrificially lead and the wife is called to sacrificially submit in the image of the Son.[207] This does not mean that the husband has a right to abuse his position. Biblically, the only time a husband would be justified in exercising his authority would be if there was a conflict in the relationship that could not be resolved. In such a scenario, the husband would be called to break the deadlock by making the decision he believes is in his wife's best interest. The authority given to him by God is only to be used to love, protect and care for his spouse. Likewise, the Father has authority over and sends the Son to earth, and the Son submits to the Father's plan. While the Trinity is certainly mirrored in the marriage covenant, in this chapter I want to focus on unpacking how human marriage reveals the eternal marriage between Jesus and the Church.

One of the stumbling blocks when attempting to comprehend this reality is gender. What does it mean for both men and women to collectively represent the bride as the Church; and how does this picture of men and women as the collective bride mesh with the idea that men also represent Jesus within marriage?

I remember sitting in youth group as a young teen and listening to the pastor describe the Church's role as the bride of Christ. The thought of me in a white dress being presented to Jesus was bizarre and I tried to put the image from my mind as quickly as possible. Seeing Jesus and me in any sort of romantic context was about the last thing I wanted to picture. Sure, I could see how the bride image could appeal to women, but for guys? Get real!

The bridal image of the Church reveals the closeness God desires with his people. A believer's role as bride is not connected to becoming feminine. Jesus refers to his Church as his bride to give words to the incredibly deep passion that he has for her.

While the bride is made up of believers from both genders, there is a sense in which women represent a type of humanity. As God protects, provides and initiates relationship with humanity through a masculine image, humanity is called to joyfully respond to the invitation as a woman would to a handsome male suitor.

It is easier for women to relate to Jesus' identity as bridegroom because God created women with hearts that long to be pursued by a man and Jesus is the ultimate pursuer. The divine romance Jesus is orchestrating draws a woman's heart in a special way as she has a piece of the equation that does not necessarily come naturally to a man. In this, women are given a special gift.

Many men are confused and turned off by notions that Jesus is in love with them. It is important to clarify that we are not to view relationship with Jesus in a sexual way. Christian men often struggle with the image of Jesus as a lover because we confuse passion with sexuality. The idea of Jesus as a bridegroom is not about sexuality, it's about his heart's desire for us. As a groom looks at his bride for the first time on their wedding day, *that* is how Jesus sees his Church. So how are men to relate to the image of Jesus as bridegroom? Let me share with you a story about how I learned to relate to this image as a man.

* * *

December 19th 2013,

The day was ending, or so I thought. It was getting late and I decided to head into the TV room in my basement and do some journaling before bed. I jotted down a few things and played a music video on TV called "Relentless" by *Hillsong United*. After, I took a seat on my black leather couch and began talking with God. As a few minutes passed, I noticed a mild frustration lingering in my gut. Here I was, spending time with the greatest being in the universe and I wasn't feeling anything. I didn't feel great, I didn't feel bad. I was irritated because in my head I knew that it was an amazing privilege to speak to God, yet my heart was disengaged. If a beautiful woman suddenly walked into the room, she would have my complete attention. My response would have been effortless. Why could I respond to a woman with such ease yet struggle to sit with God?

So I asked him. *God, if a woman walked in the room right now, I would be fully engaged. Why does it seem harder for me to connect with you than with her?* A picture then appeared in my head. I was standing behind a one-way mirror looking at a beautiful girl facing me on the other side of the glass. She was sitting in a chair not far from the mirror, talking to me. Simply looking at her was fascinating and wonderful.

But then something happened. She began to doubt. Was she *just* talking to a mirror? Perhaps no one really was on the other side? So she fell silent. I was on my feet calling out to her, *No, no, please keep going. I want to hear you.* I genuinely wanted to hear her thoughts, yet she remained quiet. A look of disappointment began to cloud her appearance. As she looked to the ground I continued to plead with her, but she did not hear me.

Then I understood.

I may not see him, I may not always feel him, but that does nothing to change his deep affections for me. He longs to hear my voice.

I began watching the music video *Love Story* by Taylor Swift. The video starts off with a Taylor exiting her school when she sees a boy sitting by a tree reading a book. As soon as he looks up at her, she has a flashback. For a split second she sees the two of them dressed in old-school fancy clothing facing each other. It almost looks like they are about to dance. Stopping in her tracks, she looks at the boy in confusion and he returns the same bewildered expression. The scene then cuts to the world Taylor saw in her flashback and we begin to see the full story. We are taken to a mansion where a dinner party is underway. Everyone is dressed in fine clothing and it is here she meets the man she saw reading under the tree. What starts with a dance quickly turns into a romance.

As the video played I tried to see myself as Taylor and the man as Jesus. Granted this was kind of weird, but my thought was, *since a bride is a picture of the Church, which I'm a part of, perhaps I can gain something by trying to see the relationship from the woman's perspective.* Picturing myself as Taylor was a stretch and when the man showed up for the dance, my eyes remained on her. There was only one person I felt any kind of desire for in the scene.

Then, like a flash of light in my mind, it suddenly clicked. I couldn't help but laugh. *Really*? I focused my gaze on her again. *How had I not seen this before*? I was overcome. It finally made sense.

Yes, I *was* Taylor in the sense that I was the bride, but I had made one crucial error. I was not meant to see the scene from her perspective. As a man, God had given me the privilege of viewing the coming marriage from *his* perspective. I was to see the romance from the position of the groom. The passionate love a man feels for a woman is a glimpse of God's radical love for his bride.

Mind explosion.

When I got this revelation I was ecstatic. This was a love I could relate to! I knew what it felt like to be captivated by a woman, and these deep emotions ultimately pointed to God's love for me. It had never quite made sense how I was supposed to relate to Jesus as his bride but now it came together. As a man, this view of Jesus as bridegroom was freeing and exciting. God was not calling me to trade in my masculinity and relate to him as a woman. Far from it. A man's intense desire for his bride gives him an insight into Jesus' love for his Church.

Still in a daze after this dawned on me, I began watching a live performance of the song. As Taylor sang, people at the edge of the stage and in the crowd were overwhelmed, jumping and reaching out to touch her while fans everywhere were recording with their phones. No one in the room doubted that she was the star. This girl had it all: looks, money, talent, fame. People in the audience were going wild for her. They intently desired her. Did God really see *me* like the crowd saw her?

Yes.

A massive smile broke across my face. God not only liked

me, he was obsessed with me. I'm *always* on his mind. He *longs* to know me. His heart beats faster when I draw close to him. He sees me as stunningly beautiful. When I sing or even just smile, he is filled with delight.

> *""The LORD your God is with you, the Mighty Warrior who saves. He will take great delight in you; in his love he will no longer rebuke you, but will rejoice over you with singing."""*
>
> (Zephaniah 3:17) [208]

On this verse Dutch Sheets writes, "[T]he word translated "rejoice"…literally means "to spin around under the influence of any violent emotion.""[209] In other words, when God looks at his beloved, he dances.

After that night I began to see the world in a new light. Two days later I was at a coffee shop with a couple of elderly ladies. As we drank our hot drinks I was elated to be spending my day with these people. Sure, their physical beauty had faded and the world wasn't interested in pursuing them, but that's not what God thought! To God, these two ladies were his beloved. When he gazes at them he sees perfect beauty. As I stared into each of their eyes, I saw passed the wrinkled faces because I knew the truth. I was sitting next to Taylor Swift.

Rest in Love

If God washes away his bride's sin and clothes her in Jesus' righteousness, it leads to some amazing conclusions for his Church. Both men and women struggle with insecurities. A man's anxiety is often rooted in the question, "Am I successful?" while a woman's worry usually stems from the question, "Am I beautiful?" God's response to his bride's questions is resoundingly clear.

Are you successful? Is Jesus successful? Absolutely! He is the embodiment of success. When God looks at you he sees success.

Are you beautiful? Is Jesus beautiful? Yes! He is the perfection of beauty. When God looks at you he sees stunning beauty.

God speaks to the deepest questions that haunt our identity and blesses us beyond our wildest dreams.

Have you ever really liked someone who didn't have a clue the way you felt for them? While they were oblivious, your heart throbbed each time you drew near to them. There was a longing that they would come to know your deep affections for them. When you felt this way, you were standing in the shadow of the greater story. In the same way, God longs for you to know his love. His heart breaks when he sees you chasing his shadow when all along he has been standing in front of you with open arms. For your entire life he has been standing patiently at your door, whispering your name.

> *""Here I am! I stand at the door and knock. If anyone hears my voice and opens the door, I will come in and eat with that person, and they with me.""*
>
> (Revelation 3:20)[210]

Key Points:

- Embracing the image of the Church as bride is not about altering one's masculinity or femininity. It is a picture revealing Jesus' passionate desire for his people.
- Women are given insight to see the coming marriage from the bride's (Church's) perspective. Men are given insight to see the coming marriage from the groom's (Jesus') perspective.
- God sees his bride as perfect. She is both successful and beautiful.

FOURTEEN

FLASHBACK TO ETERNITY

IN THE FILM *The Giver* we are taken to a dystopian society in the future. All memories of the past have been erased and a council of elders rules the community that is monitored by cameras at all times. Community members must wear assigned clothing, follow a strict curfew and take daily injections. We eventually learn that these injections limit a person's vision to black and white and remove emotions. It is a world without animals, books, music, last names, celebrities or love. Life is engineered to minimize pain and maximize equality.

Upon finishing school, the community gathers for the ceremony of advancement where the elders unveil the new career of each student finishing school. We are introduced to a young graduate named Jonas. At the ceremony the chief elder begins calling each of the graduates to the podium to announce their occupation. Tension builds as Jonas' turn approaches. Finally, when his time arrives, the chief elder skips over him as if he didn't exist. Once everyone is called, Jonas is left standing on the stage alone. The chief elder then turns to him and announces that they have selected him for a very special position. He is to be the next Receiver of Memory.

With little knowledge about his new job, the next day Jonas bikes to an old stone building at the edge of the community to begin his assignment. Inside he meets his teacher, the other Receiver of Memory called the Giver. Jonas discovers that his role is to learn the secret history of the world. He is to be exposed to the past and experience things he has never known existed. When the elders require wisdom from the past to make a decision, they will come to him for guidance.

The Giver has the ability to take Jonas into an altered state and transmit memories to him in a way that it feels as if he has personally experienced them. One of the first things the Giver reveals to his apprentice is colour. Jonas suddenly discovers that the world he has been living in goes beyond merely black and white. Soon after, the Giver shows him music for the first time by playing the piano. While Jonas stands stunned, listening to the melody, the Giver grabs his hand and imparts a memory of a wedding that took place hundreds of years earlier. Violins and tambourines play and the courtyard is filled with people dancing in celebration. Upon waking from the vision, Jonas immediately questions why anyone would want to get rid of such beautiful things.

When he learns that it is the daily injections that rob the people of colour and emotion, he begins to fake taking his medication. Suddenly he begins to develop inexplicable feelings for his friend Fiona. He dreams that the two of them are at a wedding where they run into the forest and kiss. Soon Jonas convinces Fiona to stop taking her injections and they meet the next day in a hidden location.

When they meet up, Jonas is anxious to see if the effects from her injections have worn off. He takes her hands and asks her if she feels anything. Looking intently up at him, she tells him that she doesn't have the words to describe her feeling. Then he kisses her. Having never seen or experienced a kiss, she asks him what it was. His eyes fixed on her, he tells her that there is so much more. If only she too could see the world in colour.

The day I walked into the Red Barn Market and looked into the eyes of the cashier, I knew she was seeing the world in black and white. She didn't understand the great adventure that God was calling her into. She didn't know that the reason her soul burned with love was because of the story God had written on her heart; a story that pointed to him.

* * *

Quest:
A journey made in search of something.
A long and difficult effort to find or do something.
A chivalrous enterprise in medieval romance usually involving an adventurous journey.[211]

* * *

We began our journey by examining some of the core longings of our hearts and asking the question, *where did they come from?* The first story we looked at was a universe without God. In this story we saw that love is a chemical reaction and the entire universe is destined for destruction. Next we looked at one of the most pursued artifacts of all time, the cup Jesus presented at the Last Supper known as the Holy Grail. It was suggested that the true power of the Grail was found in what it represents; that through offering the Grail at the Last Supper, Jesus was revealing the meaning of love, marriage, gender and life; that he was revealing to us another story. Yet in order to discover the true meaning of the Grail and unlock the mystery, we needed to return to the Jewish scriptures which Jesus' disciples would have known.

Throughout our journey through the Bible we learned that before the creation of the universe the eternal triune God existed in a perfect relationship of love and joy. Mankind was not created because God lacked anything, but so that he could lavish us with his amazing love. God creates Adam and Eve and marries them to offer a glimpse into the dance of love he shares in himself and to show a picture of his divine plan. Human history is one long journey towards a wedding. At this wedding, God will invite his people to share in the glorious marriage-like dance he has experienced throughout eternity. Yet tragedy strikes in the garden. Adam and Eve reject their creator and sin enters the world. But God has a plan. He will use their betrayal to unveil the depth of his love.

Two-thousand years pass and God comes to the man Abraham and tells him that all peoples on earth will be blessed through him. Although Abraham's wife is barren, a miracle child will be born who will establish God's eternal covenant. The sign God gives for this covenant is circumcision and God promises a day when he will circumcise the people's hearts, "so that you will love the Lord *your God with all you*r heart and with all your soul, that you may live."[212]

God is saying that he has a plan to purify our hearts from sin and restore us to the garden. Abraham is instructed by God to travel to a special mountain to offer his only son and, just before the sacrifice, God the Son appears to Abraham and tells him to stop.

As God promised, Abraham's descendants multiply greatly and God comes to Isaac's son Jacob and changes his name to Israel. God delivers Israel's descendants from slavery in Egypt and enters into a marriage covenant with them. Shortly after, Israel rebels and God promises a new covenant that will deal with the effects of sin.

Two-thousand years after Abraham, God sends another miracle child, a descendent of Isaac, to establish the new covenant. He is the Messiah; but more than that, he is God in the flesh. The Son is sent to earth as the perfect sacrifice to cleanse the world of sin. He presents himself as a bridegroom and offers his life as the bride price.

In his death, Jesus demonstrates his incredible love and desire to be united with us. In his resurrection, he shows us that there is hope after death. He has overcome the grave. He takes the tragedy of death and turns it into the gateway to eternal joy. Before Jesus ascends to heaven, he tells his disciples that he is going to prepare a place for them and that he will return. This is his promise. He is coming again for his bride.

* * *

> *I think the one thing I'm really afraid of is that the magic doesn't last. The butterflies and daydreams and love, all these things I hold so dear, are going to leave some day. I haven't had a relationship that's lasted forever.*
>
> – Taylor Swift[213]

* * *

This book has been about the story Jesus revealed to us through his life and the offering of the Grail. Now that we are drawing near to the end of our journey, what can we say is the meaning of love, marriage, gender and life as revealed through Jesus' life and the Grail?

Love. When Jesus offered the cup of wine to his disciples, he was showing them the ultimate expression of love by laying down his life for them. Love is not an emotion; love is a story. Love is a story because love is a person. Jesus is the embodiment of true love. Deep in our hearts is a longing for a relationship where the magic never fades and lasts forever. This is because there *is* such a thing as a perfect relationship that lasts forever. He's called God.

He wants you. He isn't simply fond of you; he *intensely* desires you. In your desire for love, God is calling out to you. *It points to me. It points to my story. Come and make it our story.*

God has written his plan and desire on our hearts: A man is captivated by a beautiful woman. He pursues her. She falls in love with him. They are married. And most importantly of all, they live happily ever after. While adults dismiss this fairy tale ending as fantasy, children embrace it with joy. Could it be that the children have had it right all along? Our yearning for this kind of relationship points to God's plan. History *is* leading to a royal wedding where there really will be a happily ever after. What then is the meaning of love? If love is God, love is a beautiful mystery we are called to enjoy and share with the world.

Marriage and Gender. When Jesus took the cup at the Last Supper and declared it the new covenant in his blood, he used the imagery of a marriage proposal. John Klein and Adam Spears write, "Each time we take communion we should remember that we are literally reaffirming our commitment to be [Jesus'] bride."[214] Marriage was created to display the inner life of God, his oneness and sacrificial love, and give us a picture of God's plan: the marriage of the bride and the Son. Ultimately, marriage is meant to glorify God.

Both genders reveal dimensions of God's heart. At the Last Supper, Jesus cast himself as the bridegroom and his disciples as his bride. Symbolically then, in this life a husband and wife are called to rehearse and offer the world a picture of the ultimate marriage. A husband is given the role of seeing the relationship from Jesus' perspective and a bride from the Church's perspective. In marriage, men are called to Jesus' example of loving, sacrificial leadership and women to Jesus' example of loving, sacrificial submission. When each gender embraces these roles in the marriage covenant, we see a glimpse of the inner life of God. By embracing our gender, we give glory to God. Ultimately, gender is about glorifying God.

Life. What is the purpose of our existence? John Piper says, "The chief end of man is to glorify God by enjoying Him forever."[215] Life is about giving God glory. And how do we do that?

By enjoying him.

A husband's greatest satisfaction is to see his wife completely delighted in him. This is God's desire. This is why he offered his life as our bride price. He knew his death would offer us the joy of being delighted in him forever. This is the meaning of life: to give ourselves completely to Love.

* * *

The music video to the song *Love Story* begins with a girl who has a flashback after glancing into the eyes of a man. In an instant she sees snapshots of a romance between them that somehow happened in the distant past. As the song nears its conclusion, there is a moment when it seems the man has left forever, but, then, he suddenly appears. We return from the vision to the real world and see the man sitting under the tree begin to approach Taylor. He comes close to her and the two of them look deeply into each other's eyes. As they stand face to face, everything seems to click. They are part of a much larger story; a love story for the ages. It all seems very impossible, but in their hearts they know. This was real. Their lives had been leading to this moment.

* * *

The Prestige

40-25-6

You are standing on the outskirts of a great white city. On each side of you is a landscape with lakes and mountains too beautiful to describe. In front of you is a golden bridge without railings that seems to float high above the valley below. The path leads to two giant doors, larger than any you have ever seen. To your right, you notice a person dressed in white.

"It's time," the man says warmly as he motions for you to walk across the bridge.

Your heart skips a beat.

Instinctively you know where this path leads. The bridge is long and will take a few minutes to cross. As you take your first steps, you begin to hear music, what sounds like ten thousand orchestras playing in harmony. Goosebumps flood your body as the melodies surround you. With each step forward the music grows more intense until you finally reach the towering doors. The source of the sound is clearly coming from behind them. Then, together, the mighty doors slowly open.

You swallow.

Amazingly, you feel the music enter inside you. The song is directed to you. It is more exciting and beautiful than anything you have experienced and fills your body with warmth. As the doors part, a wave of light shines through. You look down the massive white hall to see a man standing in the distance. He is the source of the song filling the air. A peace unlike anything you have known surrounds you. And then it happens. He calls to you.

Your name.

A smile breaks across your face. Suddenly the two of you are racing towards each other. You run into his arms and feel his strong embrace. As you pull back you look into his eyes for the first time. Tears are streaming down both of your faces.

You know.

Beyond a shadow of doubt, *you know*. The moment your eyes meet, your life flashes before you. In an instant, each moment of your journey plays in front of you: moments of joy, hardship, peace, passion, pain, despair. When you took your first breath, your first birthday, your first day of school, when you first moved from home, all the tragedies you encountered, the mundane car rides to and from work, when you saw your spouse for the first time, the last time you said goodbye to your parents, to all the ordinary days of preparing meals and cleaning the yard, you see it all in that moment. But now it is all displayed before you as a stunning canvas. The many moments in life you looked back on with regret and frustration have been changed into something beautiful. You see how God took what was ordinary and broken and sculpted it into something amazing.

All the confusion, all the pain, all your unanswered questions melted when you looked into his eyes. The puzzle pieces of your life have been assembled into a larger story. As you look upon the canvas made of the moments of your existence, the picture is unmistakable. It reveals a picture of *this* moment. You see Jesus' embrace of you. Throughout your stained and jumbled life, God has been preparing a canvas leading you here. All your doubts and fears have disappeared. All you feel is love. You suddenly understand how all your longings on earth pointed to their fulfillment here. But then you see your life canvas again and notice something else. The picture itself forms a giant puzzle piece. You see Jesus take it in his hand and place it on his heart. It's a perfect fit. You hear a voice inside of you. *Welcome home.*

With his arms still holding you, he pulls back to look into your eyes. A tear falls. This is the moment he has been waiting for. Gently he says to you, "You were never the sideshow. To me, you have always been the main event." What feels like an energizing wave of electricity fills your body as the gravity of his words sink into your heart. Filled with emotion he looks at you and says, "I will never forget your name. It is forever written on my heart."

* * *

Deep down, you have always known you were meant for something great. It is a feeling that is often difficult to explain, but it lingers in the core of your being. *There must be more to life than this.*

God is calling you.

God is in the process of writing the greatest love story of all time and he is inviting you to join him at the center. While the invitation is not always obvious, it is woven into the desires of our hearts. In our songs and art is a desire for adventure and romance. It is the shadow of God's overarching plan. When we see movies where a superhero saves the world and meets a beautiful woman, we are filled with a sense of wonder. *Am I worthy of being pursued?*

God is calling you.

When we see William Wallace charging the battlefield in a fury, our hearts are filled with inspiration and passion. *Would anyone fight for me like that?*

God is calling you.

When we see Jenna marry the one who's always loved her, we smile and our hearts are warmed. *Will my story have a happy ending?*

God is calling you.

When Jesus tells the story of the son who disgraced his father and wasted his inheritance, we feel the son should be punished. Yet the father immediately invites him back into the family and throws a massive party. The father always loved his son, despite his rebellion. He was always waiting for his return. *Could God really love me after what I've done?*

God is calling you.

When Jesus approaches the Samaritan woman at the well, she is the last person he should be associating with. But not only does he speak to her, he invites her into an adventure beyond her wildest dreams. Will you accept his invitation?

God is calling you.

You were never the sideshow. You have always held God's eye. His heart aches that you would know his love. All this time he has been waiting for you. Throughout your life, he has been calling your name. You may not have understood the words were his at the time, but looking back the image becomes clear. From the beginning he has been there, calling you.

Do you see it? I've been here all along.

And when you hear the song, remember…

You Belong With Me.

AFTERWORD

WHAT DO YOU believe? Perhaps you are far from convinced that the story revealed through the Bible is true. I encourage you to do your own investigation. That's what my good friend Randy did when he experienced doubts about what he believed (you can read more about his story in our book *Thrive: A Guide for Life's Journey*). Randy agrees that his choice to investigate the evidence was one of the most significant decisions he has made and it has transformed his life. If you are interested in examining some of the evidence for God, three books that I have personally found helpful are, *The Reason for God* by Timothy Keller, *The Case for Christ* by Lee Strobel and *Mere Christianity* by C.S. Lewis.

If you *do* believe the story, what's next? Many people put their faith in God and then carry on with their lives. Sure, God is a part of their life, they go to church, read the Bible and pray every now and then, but that's about it.

God longs for *so much more*.

There are many people who believe their relationship with God is going great simply because they attend church. How do you think your spouse would feel if you committed to spending two hours with them each Sunday and then practically ignored them for the rest of the week? It is possible to spend your entire life with someone and not love them. However, when we truly love someone, we naturally desire to know them. So how do we love God? If we try to love him on our own strength we are setting ourselves up for failure. Our love for God flows from his love for us.

When we rest in the truth of his extravagant affections towards us, we are empowered by his grace to live out a life of love. The key is to continually rest in the truths about who God is and who we are in light of what he has done. As humans we are easily distracted and need frequent reminding. Here are some truths you can rest in as a believer:

God is good. He uses *everything* for your ultimate good. (Romans 8:28).

You are forgiven. When you accepted God's invitation, all your sin was transferred to Jesus when he hung on the cross and you received his righteousness (Romans 3:22, Ephesians 1:7).

You are successful. When God sees you, he sees Jesus' perfectly successful life (2 Corinthians 5:21).

You are beautiful. When God looks at you, he sees Jesus' perfect beauty (Song of Songs 4:7).

You are God's child. God loves you as a good and perfect father (Luke 15:20).

You are God's bride. God longs for you with the passion of a bridegroom (Luke 22:20).

You are God's favourite. When God looks upon you, he sees his favourite one (John 15:9).

Refresh yourself in these truths. You cannot earn your way to favour with God. Your position in his heart is a gift given by his grace. When you allow the Spirit to makes these truths real in your heart, you naturally desire to reflect God's radical love.

How does one live a lifestyle where they are constantly reminded of these truths? This is not about setting up a formula, but engaging with a person. It's about relationship. One thing you will be required to sacrifice in making any relationship work is time. How much time do you spend with God? By asking yourself this question you can probably gauge the health of your relationship. Do you set aside time to specifically spend with him to pray, read scripture and worship? If the first thing that comes to your mind upon hearing this is dread, you need to be touched by God's love for you. Ask the Spirit to open your heart to his affections for you. Many people don't know where to start when it comes to spending time with God. Simply have a conversation with him. As you read the Bible, ask him questions. Journal about what he is revealing to you. Throw on some worship music. Remember, a spouse doesn't want you to block out 15 minutes to sit down with them each day; they want to live life with you. God wants to live life alongside you. What a privilege! As you go throughout your day, have a running dialogue with him. Tell him your thoughts, feelings and fears and remind yourself of his goodness.

The movie *Gladiator* ends with a battle in the Coliseum between Maximus and the Roman Emperor Commodus. Maximus, a former Roman General, is betrayed by Commodus who orders the burning and crucifixion of his wife and son. At the film's conclusion, Maximus defeats his foe but is mortally wounded from a dagger Commodus strikes him with before the fight. As he begins to drift out of consciousness, Maximus sees himself walking to the gates of his home. As he walks through the field he sees two people standing on the road in the distance. It is his wife and son. As he approaches, he sees his son come running towards him. They are about to be reunited. As Jesus hung on the cross about to die, I am sure he was looking towards his prize. He saw the reunion his death would bring. He longed to be reunited with the ones he loved.

God's eye has been on you for a long time. He won't force you to come to the wedding, but he's proposing to you, earnestly.

What are you living for? Are you living for money, sex, marriage, family, retirement, popularity or your career? Do not get distracted with these things: they are not the main event. You may think you are on a stage performing for an audience that isn't interested, but this is not true. You have an audience of one who has been pursuing you throughout your life.

God whispers to us in our longings and shouts to us through his word that there is more to reality than this life. It is insane to be captivated by someone's shadow while ignoring the person. The shadow points to a greater reality. Yet many of us fix our eyes on love and romance in this life, oblivious to the source. We chase the shadow of God while he stands next to us calling our name. There is more to life than chasing a shadow. Life is a quest not ultimately about finding love, but finding the one who *is* Love. I hope that our journey together has awakened a passion within you, for Love.

Z

MIRACLES

GRACE JOGGED OVER to the green bench in McMichael Park and sat down. She felt refreshed after a casual run through the neighbourhood. It was nothing too strenuous this evening because she didn't want to wear herself out for the dance. Near her feet she spotted a patch of daisies on the grass. She could remember picking them here years ago as a young girl. She and Eleanor had run through this field many times while growing up. Grace had always looked forward to experiencing the world as an adult, but there was definitely something special about those earlier days. They had frolicked through this field laughing, without a worry in the world. Life had been so simple and joyful.

She reached for her phone and found the song "Let it Happen" by *United Pursuit*. Her eyes closed as the music played. Scenes from her childhood flashed before her while she rested in the sound. Silently her lips began moving with the lyrics. Over time, the words became a whisper under her breath. Finally, as the minutes passed, the whisper grew into a soft but clear song. It was then that her eyes opened. Breathing deeply she stood to her feet, looking to the clouds with a satisfied smile. It only took her a couple of minutes to walk to the other side of the park. In the corner by the road was a blue sign that read,

Welcome to
McMichael Park,
East Falls,
Established 1929

This park had been here for a long time. *1929.* If she remembered correctly that was the year Grace Kelly was born. She too would have grown up playing in this park. Crossing the sidewalk, she came to stand in front of the house. How many times had she stopped here? For years a certain enchantment had continued to draw her to this place. She had often wondered what it was that kept her coming back. Now, as the song was coming to a close, it was beginning to dawn on her.

Yes, it was the whisper in her heart.

After returning home she showered and prepared herself for the evening. She put on the new blue dress she had bought and went out to her car. It was a short drive into downtown East Falls where she parked and began walking to the event. She was running the dance workshop along with another girl this year and she had to be there early. As she approached the scene she could see the pleasant blue glow from the lights strung up along the top of the bridge.

Once the event got underway the bridge was flooded with hundreds of people who had come to dance. The hours rolled by quickly as a steady stream of people filled the small roped off section that was designated for the lessons. Once 11:30 finally arrived, both Grace and her co-instructor Ginger were tired from teaching pretty well non-stop for the last four and a half hours. After tidying up, Ginger went off with one of her friends and Grace made her way to the end of the bridge where the food trucks were parked. She ordered some fries and ate them hastily. Making her way back to the dance floor, she hoped to catch the last few songs as the final band finished for the night. The crowds had begun to thin by this hour but there were still lots of people dancing. Shortly after reaching the edge of the dance floor she heard a voice from behind.

"Grace."

When she turned around and saw who it was, her heart jumped.

It was Jack.

She hadn't seen Jack since high school. Although several years had passed, he was still handsome as ever. "Jack," she said, taken aback at his sudden appearance. "Wow, you look great."

"Thanks," he said shyly. "You too."

"It's been ages."

"Yeah."

Grace noticed the young girl clutching his hand at his side. "So what brings you out here tonight?"

"Well," he motioned with his hand, "this one really wanted to come out to this." He shrugged, "So here we are."

Grace nodded and bent down in front of the child. She

had long light brown hair and blue eyes that seemed to sparkle. "And what's your name?"

"I'm Jane," she replied with a big smile.

"What a pretty name." Grace quickly glanced up at Jack. "And how old are you Jane?"

"Five," she held out her hand, displaying her fingers.

"Wow, five years old." Grace got back up and looked at Jack.

"I hope you don't think I'm a terrible person for keeping her out this late. I made her have a nap before supper and I'm sure she will sleep well tonight."

"I'm sure she will."

"But yeah, we're just about to head but I saw you and figured we'd come and say hi."

"I'm glad you did. So you've been keeping well?"

"Yeah," he looked over at Jane, "been keeping well. Well as to be expected. How about you?"

"Good," she nodded, "got a job doing some admin work at the university up the way, but yeah, things have been good."

"That's great, and you've been enjoying it?"

"Yeah, I have. It's not too far from my place, and the staff are nice."

"Awesome." His eyes were fixed on her. "You been up to anything else?"

Her stomach fluttered. Should she say? "Well, I've been doing a bit of writing. Just published a book."

"Wow, a book? That's really something. What's it about?"

"Oh, goodness," she ran a finger through the side of

her hair and her eyes dropped to the ground, "how to describe it."

"Is it fiction?"

She looked up at him, pausing. "Kind of," her eyes squinted. "It's labelled fiction, but I guess that's because I figured no one would believe me otherwise."

He looked at her curiously. "So it isn't fiction?"

A smile came to her face. "You know what, I think I might have a copy in my car. I could give it to you, if you're interested in reading it, and you can decide for yourself."

"Totally, I'd love to read your book."

"Okay, well I'm just parked this way."

The three of them walked off the bridge towards where Grace was parked.

"So what inspired you to write a book?"

Grace took a deep breath. "Well, it's a bit of a story. I guess it all started here in East Falls. I somehow ended up in Canada for school and met someone up there and, well, it's a long story. But a bunch of stuff happened and one day while I was working, this strange guy gives me this book, and it was all just so incredible what happened that I knew I had to share the story, in a way that somehow made sense. I know I'm not making sense right now, but if you read the book, well, yeah. You'll just have to read it."

They approached her car and she unlocked the passenger door. She climbed inside and reached for the book between the seats. "Here," she handed it to him.

Jack examined the cover. "*My Promise*. Hmm, sounds intriguing. I really look forward to reading it, and that's saying something because I'm not a big reader." He smiled awkwardly through a couple seconds of silence. "Well," he breathed in, "I guess I should be getting this one home, but it was good seeing you."

"It was good seeing you too, Jack." She could genuinely say those words without a hint of animosity. It was a wonderful thing.

Still facing her, he took a step away, but then he stopped. His lips were pressed together and his head was slightly turned to the side. "Grace," his gaze soon drifting to the ground, "that message you sent me way back." He paused and looked up at her. "Thank you."

A soft smile grew on her face. "You know, everything happens for a reason and I've seen firsthand that God can take the worst moments and transform them into something beautiful." She was almost surprised at how the words came to her so naturally. "Maybe one of these days we can go grab a donut or something, for old time's sake."

His head tilted up and the stiffness in his posture melted. "Yeah," he gestured with his hand, "yeah I'd really like that. I would love that. And we can discuss your book."

"Sure, well, call me sometime. That is if you remember my number?"

"Oh, I remember, and I just might do that."

She smiled. "Alright, I'll be seeing you then."

He stepped back. "Thanks, Grace. Okay"

She waved and watched them walk away. Jane was such an adorable little thing and Grace couldn't help but wonder who the mother was. Most of all, she wondered what he would think of the book. The thought of meeting with him again made her nervous and excited.

Once they were out of sight she walked back to the bridge and returned to the edge of the dance floor. The band was now playing their last song. She breathed in deeply and gazed out into the crowd of people dancing in front of her. It was then that she noticed someone standing near the band on the other side of the dance floor. A chill ran through her. She blinked. How was this happening?

Wearing a red blazer he was looking directly at her with his characteristic smile. As their eyes met, an overflow of bewildered excitement flooded her. She couldn't describe it, but somehow she could hear in her heart what he wanted to say. As she looked into his eyes she knew he was proud of her. He had never left her, and he never would.

His head calmly nodded, as if to confirm it was true.

A couple dancing moved in front of her, briefly blocking her view of him. When they passed by, he had disappeared. Grace immediately stepped onto the dance floor and frantically looked side to side, but he was gone.

Her heart racing, she stood still, astonished. Eventually she made her way to a quiet spot at the side of the bridge. Gazing down she could clearly see the blue lights from the side of the bridge reflect on the water.

She realized the absence of the music. The band had stopped playing.

All was still.

A song began to play on the speakers. It was familiar. She knew this song, didn't she? When the lyrics began, it came to her. It was *See You Again* by Carrie Underwood. As she listened to the lyrics a tear fell from her eye. This had to be more than coincidence.

It was then she noticed them in the water. They were everywhere. She laughed and looked up.

Stars filled the sky.

Checking the time it was exactly midnight.

Then, it was as if something clicked in her mind and she finally understood.

Her name. She shook her head in awe.

Her real name was *Grace Kelly*. It had always been her name, yet only now did she truly see it.

She had never been just another girl. She had been chosen, and now she was royalty. Her wildest dreams had come more than true. In his eyes, she was the most famous and adored person in the world. She was reminded of the verse the pastor had talked about on Sunday. He had said that grace wasn't just an idea, but a person, quoting John 1:17. *Grace and truth came through Jesus Christ*. She thought back to when she had changed her name. All along it had really been him. *He* had changed her name. He had given her *his* name: Grace.

Whispering into the night sky, she spoke her name aloud for the first time. The dream had become reality. Indeed, it had always been reality.

Suddenly she was brought back to the time he had dropped her off at her house after taking her to the gardens. That night he had asked her a question, and she hadn't been able to give a clear answer. But now she knew.

Looking up at the stars, she nodded. "Yes, I do believe."

WE DANCE

Cook, Amanda, and Steffany Gretzinger, writers. Bethel Music. 2013.

ACKNOWLEDGMENTS

A big thanks to all my friends and family who took the time to give me their feedback on my work.

Holly Conklin is an editing superstar. Don't let her introversion deceive you into thinking her mind is not full of ideas because it's packed with creative genius. If you need any serious editing done, you should hire her.

Daniela Schnetzler is a reading machine, literally. She reads at least a book per week and her experience with words was on display in the help she provided.

Nikita Reimer is an extremely fun person to be around and amazing with details. Thanks to her keen eye she was able to comb through my manuscripts and greatly improve them.

Amanda Ingram is one of those people that always brings you a smile when you are with her. Thanks for your feedback!

Randy Conklin, I'm glad to have a scientist friend who can analyse my work.

Tina Bergum, Rob Friesen, Robin Rasmussen and Siobhan Gilbert were also kind enough to help me with editing. Thank you all for your time!

Auntie Weez, you trained me well in life and I'm grateful for your insights and support.

My parents, sister and grandparents, thank you for your input and encouragement. Love you all very much!

Finally, thank you Jesus for giving me the strength and endurance to see this project through. You are my inspiration and joy.

NOTES

Chapter 1: The Main Event

1. “Taylor Swift Net Worth.” The Richest. http://www.therichest.com/celebnet-worth/celeb/singer/taylor-swift-net-worth.
2. Stewart, Thomas. “Which 5 Book Genres Make The Most Money?” THERICHEST. 2014. http://www.therichest.com/rich-list/which-5-book-genres-make-the-most-money/5.
3. If you want to learn more about how men and women’s brains are different, I recommend Dr. Louann Brizendine’s books *The Male Brain* and *The Female Brain*.
4. Eldredge, John. “Wild at Heart.” In *Wild at Heart: Discovering the Secret of a Man’s Soul*, 9-10. Nashville, Tennessee: T. Nelson, 2001.
5. Eldredge, John, and Stasi Eldredge. “The Heart of a Woman.” In *Captivating: Unveiling the Mystery of a Woman’s Soul*, 8-12. Orange, California: T. Nelson, 2005.
6. Goudreau, Jenna. “Disney Princess Tops List Of The 20 Best-Selling Entertainment Products.” Forbes. 2012. http://www.forbes.com/sites/jenna-goudreau/2012/09/17/disney-princess-tops-list-of-the-20-best-selling-entertainment-products.
7. Taylor, Swift. *RED*. 2012.
8. Macpherson, Alex. “Taylor Swift: ‘I Want to Believe in Pretty Lies’” The Guardian, 18 Oct. 2012. Web. http://www.theguardian.com/music/2012/oct/18/taylor-swift-want-believe-pretty-lies.
9. Simon Usborne. “Why the Holy Grail Is the Ultimate Unattainable Object.” Independent, April 1, 2014. http://www.independent.co.uk/voices/faith/why-the-holy-grail-is-the-ultimate-unattainable-object-9231235.html.
10. Ibid
11. http://saddleridgehoard.com.
12. Luke 22:20.
13. “Quest.” Merriam-Webster. http://www.merriam-webster.com/dictionary/quest.
14. “Best Selling Book of Non-fiction.” Guinness World Records. http://www.

guinnessworldrecords.com/world-records/best-selling-book-of-non-fiction.

Chapter 2: Before the Beginning

15. Psalm 93:2.
16. 1 John 4:8.
17. What is true love? I like author Brad Henning's definition: Love is choosing the highest good for the other person.
18. For more on the Trinity, see "Father, Son and Holy Spirit: Relationships, Roles, and Relevance" by Bruce Ware.
19. Lewis, C. S. "Good Infection." In *The Complete C.S. Lewis Signature Classics*, 143. San Francisco, Calif., New York: HarperOne, 2002.
20. Keller, Timothy. "The Dance of God." In *The Reason for God: Belief in an Age of Skepticism*. New York, New York: Dutton, 2008.
21. Unless cited otherwise, Bible verses are from the New Living Translation.
22. Comer, John Mark. "What's It For?" In *Loveology: God, Love, Sex, Marriage, and the Never-Ending Story of Male and Female*, 51. Kindle ed. Grand Rapids, Michigan: Zondervan, 2013.
23. Ibid, 61.
24. http://biblehub.com/interlinear/psalms/33-20.htm.
25. "עלָצֵ." Blue Letter Bible. https://www.blueletterbible.org/lang/lexicon/lexicon.cfm?Strongs=H6763&t=NLT.
26. Erre, M. (2013, October 1). What God Has Joined Together. Retrieved from http://www.evfreefullerton.com/blog/sermons/god-joined-together.
27. Comer, John Mark. "What's It For?" In *Loveology: God, Love, Sex, Marriage, and the Never-Ending Story of Male and Female*, 22. Kindle ed. Grand Rapids, Michigan: Zondervan, 2013.
28. Brezina, G. Why Did God Create Humanity? Retrieved from http://www.cftministry.org/resources/articles/article_why.html
29. Deuteronomy 6:4 (English Standard Version).
30. It is a fact that married people have sex more frequently than people who are unmarried and report the highest levels of sexual satisfaction. If marriage is a picture of the permanent love and unity of God in the Trinity, and sex is designed to reflect that love and unity, then it makes sense that God designed the best sex to be found within the lifelong commitment of marriage. For more stats on the benefits of marriage, see the book *The Case for Marriage* by Linda Waite and Maggie Gallagher.
31. "Male and Female Complementarity and the Image of God." May 1, 2002. http://cbmw.org/uncategorized/male-and-female-complementarity-and-the-image-of-god.
32. West, Christopher. "Mutual Fascination with the Body." In *Heaven's Song: Sexual Love as It Was Meant to Be*, 58. West Chester, Pennsylvania: Ascension Press, 2008.
33. See Revelation 12:9.
34. New American Standard Exhaustive Concordance. http://biblehub.com/

greek/264.htm.

35. Keller, Timothy. "The Insider and the Outcast." In *Encounters with Jesus: Unexpected Answers to Life's Biggest Questions*, 35. New York, New York: Dutton, 2013.
36. Smith's Bible Dictionary https://www.blueletterbible.org/search/Dictionary/viewTopic.cfm?topic=BT0002094

Chapter 3: Journey to a New Beginning

37. Jewish Historian Josephus also wrote that Sarai was Abram's niece. For further notes on the Iscah-Sarai connection, see Hebbe Gustaf Clemens', "Universal History." In *An Universal History, in a Series of Letters: Being a Complete and Impartial Narrative of the Most Remarkable Events of All Nations from the Earliest Period to the Present Time*, Etc, 15. Vol. II. New York, New York: Dewitt and Davenport, 1848.
38. Reasons for identifying the angel as God in this verse are as follows: 1. In verse 10 it is the angel who says he will give Hagar many descendants. 2. Moses, the author of Genesis, identifies the angel as God in verse 13. 3. Hagar identifies the angel as God in verse 13. For more, see commentary on Genesis 16:7 from the Geneva Study Bible aned Gill's Exposition of the Entire Bible and Adam Clarke's Commentary. http://biblehub.com/commentaries/genesis/16-7.htm.
39. Genesis 16:14 is the second time the Hebrew word for well is used, but it is the first time this word is used to speak of an actual well. The first time this word is used is in Genesis 14:10 where it is rendered "tar pits".
40. See notes on Genesis 17:5 in Andrew Wommack's Living Commentary.
41. See notes of Genesis 17:15 in Matthew Poole's Commentary. http://biblehub.com/commentaries/genesis/17-15.htm.
42. Isaac means "laughter". See Easton's Bible dictionary. https://www.blueletterbible.org/search/Dictionary/viewTopic.cfm?topic=ET0001894.
43. See Deuteronomy 10:16, Deuteronomy 30:6, Jeremiah 4:4, Jeremiah 9:26 and Romans 2:29.
44. English Standard Version.
45. McLaughlin, Ra. "Circumcision and Women." http://thirdmill.org/answers/answer.asp/file/40447.
46. Keller, Timothy, and Kathy Keller. "Sex and Marriage." In *The Meaning of Marriage: Facing the Complexities of Commitment with the Wisdom of God*, 236. New York, NY: Dutton, 2011.
47. Genesis 17:19b NLT.

Chapter 4: Mysteries in the Desert

48. English Standard Version.
49. Notice the pain that results from Abraham and Sarah trying to work around God's plan. Sarah's desire for a child causes her to give her servant Hagar to Abraham to produce an heir because she believes God does not want

her to conceive. But this is not true. God's plan all along is for Sarah to have a child, yet Sarah does not believe God is good. It is this lack of belief that causes her to initiate the events which lead to pain and frustration for both her and Abraham.

50. See Hebrews 11:19.
51. English Standard Version.
52. See Clarke's Commentary on Gen 22:19. http://biblehub.com/commentaries/clarke/genesis/22.htm.
53. See Genesis 22:11 in Clarke's Commentary and Andrew Wommack's Living commentary.
54. English Standard Version.
55. See Genesis 24:2 in Clarke's Commentary. http://biblehub.com/commentaries/clarke/genesis/24.htm.
56. "The Camels." http://www.nationalgeographic.com/weepingcamel/thecamels.html.
57. "Rebekah meaning." Abarim Publications. http://www.abarim-publications.com/Meaning/Rebekah.html#.V6JwZbgrKUl.
58. "All the Women of the Bible." Bible Gateway. https://www.biblegateway.com/resources/all-women-bible/Rebekah-Rebecca.
59. See Genesis 25:11.

Chapter 5: The Marriage Contract

60. The nation of Israel came from the descendants of Jacob, the son of Isaac, the son of Abraham.
61. See Clarke's Commentary on Exodus 20:1. http://biblehub.com/commentaries/clarke/exodus/20.htm.
62. English Standard Version.
63. For an outline of the ancient Jewish wedding traditions, see the following link: www.trackingbibleprophecy.com/jewish_wedding.php.
64. "The Ketubah—Marriage Contract." http://www.chabad.org/library/article_cdo/aid/477336/jewish/The-Ketubah-Marriage-Contract.htm.
65. Jacobs, Louis. "The Ketubah, or Marriage Contract." http://www.myjewishlearning.com/article/the-ketubah-or-marriage-contract.
66. See Clark's Commentary on Exodus 19:4.
67. Slonim, Rivkah. "The Mikvah." http://www.chabad.org/theJewishWoman/article_cdo/aid/1541/jewish/The-Mikvah.htm.
68. See Exodus 29:4 and 30:17-21 for details.
69. See Clarke's Commentary on Exodus 30:20.
70. Slonim, Rivkah. "The Mikvah." http://www.chabad.org/theJewishWoman/article_cdo/aid/1541/jewish/The-Mikvah.htm.
71. Pitre, Brant. "The Divine Love Story." In *Jesus the Bridegroom: The Greatest Love Story Ever Told*, 10-11. Kindle ed. Random House, 2014.
72. See Clarke's Commentary on Jeremiah 2:2.
73. The English Standard Version translates this verse as: "When I passed by you again and saw you, behold, you were at the age for love, and I spread

the corner of my garment over you and covered your nakedness; I made my vow to you and entered into a covenant with you, declares the Lord God, and you became mine." The phrase, "I spread the corner of my garment over you" is a direct allusion to a Jewish custom used as a wedding proposal. See Ruth 3:9 and Clarke's commentary on Ezekiel 16:8.

74. See Jamieson-Fausset-Brown Bible Commentary on Song of Songs 1:1. http://biblehub.com/commentaries/songs/1-1.htm.

Chapter 6: Foreshadows

75. The Prophet Marries a Prostitute - Part 1. Performed by Ravi Zacharias. September 24, 2014. https://www.youtube.com/watch?v=s0N9azDcgnE&list=TLOeL7dr5uOiZpfdbmCxc_1prh1GYltpFc.
76. Baal was a god the Israelites worshiped and offered child sacrifices to. God comments on this practice in Jeremiah 19:5 saying, "They have built pagan shrines to Baal, and there they burn their sons as sacrifices to Baal. I have never commanded such a horrible deed; it never even crossed my mind to command such a thing!"
77. English Standard Version.
78. English Standard Version.
79. See also Ezekiel 11:19.
80. See Gill's Exposition of the Entire Bible on Jeremiah 31:33. http://biblehub.com/commentaries/jeremiah/31-33.htm.
81. See Easton's Bible Dictionary. http://www.biblestudytools.com/dictionary/messiah. https://www.blueletterbible.org/search/Dictionary/viewTopic.cfm?topic=ET0002515.
82. See "Messiah" in the International Standard Bible Encyclopedia. http://www.biblestudytools.com/dictionary/messiah.
83. See Matthew Poole's Commentary on Michah 5:2. http://biblehub.com/commentaries/micah/5-2.htm.
84. English Standard Version.
85. See "Immanuel" in Smith's Bible Dictionary. http://www.biblestudytools.com/dictionary/emmanuel. https://www.blueletterbible.org/search/Dictionary/viewTopic.cfm?topic=BT0002066
86. Isaiah 49:6 in *Barnes' Notes on the Bible* identifies this verse as referring to the Messiah. http://biblehub.com/commentaries/isaiah/49-6.htm.
87. New International Version.
88. Steffen, Daniel. "The Messianic Banquet and the Eschatology of Matthew." June 1, 2004. https://bible.org/article/messianic-banquet-and-eschatology-matthew.
89. See Genesis 12:3.
90. Pitre, Brant. "The Divine Love Story." In *Jesus the Bridegroom: The Greatest Love Story Ever Told*, 41. Kindle ed. Random House, 2014.

Chapter 7: The Father's Heart

91. The Greek word translated "testament" in the Bible is "diathēkē". This same word is most often translated "covenant" in the Bible.
92. "Vine's Expository Dictionary of New Testament Words: Jesus." Blue Letter Bible. https://www.blueletterbible.org/search/Dictionary/viewTopic.cfm?topic=VT0001543.
93. See Isaiah 7:14 and Micah 5:2.
94. See Barnes' Notes on the Bible for Luke 15:22.

Chapter 8: Blood and Water

95. English Standard Version.
96. See Luke 1:17.
97. "John meaning." Abarim Publications. http://www.abarim-publications.com/Meaning/John.html#.U8r18-NdVIE.
98. John 1:14-17 says, *"And the Word became flesh and dwelt among us, and we have seen his glory, glory as of the only Son from the Father, full of grace and truth.* [15] *(John bore witness about him, and cried out, "This was he of whom I said, 'He who comes after me ranks before me, because he was before me.'")* [16] *For from his fullness we have all received, grace upon grace.* [17] *For the law was given through Moses; grace and truth came through Jesus Christ."* (ESV) In verse 17, John states that the law (the Ten Commandments/old covenant) was given through Moses. He then contrasts the Ten Commandments with Jesus who brings "grace" and "truth." The new covenant Jesus comes to establish is a covenant of grace.
99. See Barnes' Notes on the Bible for Matthew 3:2. http://biblehub.com/commentaries/barnes/matthew/3.htm.
100. See "baptizó" in Thayer's Greek Lexicon. http://biblehub.com/greek/907.htm.
101. See Barnes' Notes on the Bible for Matthew 3:6. http://biblehub.com/nasb/matthew/3-6.htm.
102. See John 1:19-27 and Clarke's Commentary on John 1:25. http://biblehub.com/commentaries/clarke/john/1.htm.
103. Kohler, Kaufmann. "Birth, New." Jewish Encyclopedia. http://www.jewishencyclopedia.com/contribs/563.
104. "You Must Be Born Again." HaDavar. http://www.hadavar.org/getting-to-know-god/you-must-be-born-again.
105. "Jewish Practices & Rituals: Mikveh." 2008. http://www.jewishvirtuallibrary.org/jsource/Judaism/mikveh.html.
106. We know that a purification of a bride before marriage was an established practice during this time and Ephesians 5:26 makes an allusion to this. See Barnes Notes on the Bible for Ephesians 5:26. http://biblehub.com/commentaries/ephesians/5-26.htm.
107. See Exodus 30:17-21 and Clarke's Commentary on Exodus 30:20. http://biblehub.com/commentaries/clarke/exodus/30.htm.
108. Mark 1:4 and Luke 3:3 show that one of the reasons John baptised was to

demonstrate a repentance from sin.

109. John 1:31b, brackets mine.
110. See Barnes' Notes on the Bible on John 1:29. http://biblehub.com/commentaries/john/1-29.htm.
111. For more details on Passover preparation, see Exodus 12.
112. By referring to Jesus as a lamb, there is also an echo of the prophecy about the Messiah in Isaiah 53. Verse seven reads, "*He was oppressed and treated harshly, yet he never said a word. He was led like a lamb to the slaughter. And as a sheep is silent before the shearers, he did not open his mouth.*"
113. See Pulpit Commentary on Exodus 29:4. http://biblehub.com/commentaries/pulpit/exodus/29.htm.
114. See Barnes' Notes on the Bible for John 2:1. http://biblehub.com/commentaries/john/2-1.htm.
115. English Standard Version.
116. Keller, Timothy. The Wedding Party. Kindle ed. Penguin Group, 2013. (Kindle Location 64).
117. Pitre, Brant. "The Divine Love Story." In *Jesus the Bridegroom: The Greatest Love Story Ever Told*, 43-44. Kindle ed. Random House, 2014.
118. Keller, Timothy. The Wedding Party. Kindle ed. Penguin Group, 2013. (Kindle Locations 66-68, 147-149).
119. When Mary says to Jesus, "They have no wine," she is implicitly asking Jesus to do something. See Andrew Wommack's Living Commentary on John 2:3.
120. Pitre, Brant. "The Divine Love Story." In *Jesus the Bridegroom: The Greatest Love Story Ever Told*, 44. Kindle ed. Random House, 2014.
121. See Barnes' Notes on the Bible for John 2:4. http://biblehub.com/commentaries/barnes/john/2.htm.
122. See John 12:27, 13:1 and 17:1.
123. New International Version.
124. English Standard Version.
125. These jars would have been used for conducting mikveh/baptism. One form of mikveh was to fill a tank with 40 seahs of water (around 120 gallons) for immersion. The jars at the wedding would have held more than enough water to accommodate this (See article "Water Pots for Purification" in *The Chronological Study Bible (NKJV)* (2008) Pg. 1097.) Another form of mikveh that the jars may have been used for was for the cleansing of hands before eating. Mark 7:3-4 in Young's Literal Translation says, "for the Pharisees, and all the Jews, if they do not wash the hands to the wrist, do not eat, holding the tradition of the elders, [4] and, [coming] from the market-place, if they do not baptize themselves, they do not eat; and many other things there are that they received to hold, baptisms of cups, and pots, and brazen vessels, and couches." (See also Young's Literal Translation of Luke 11:37-39).

Chapter 9: An Unlikely Invitation

126. See Clarke's Commentary on John 3:36. http://biblehub.com/commentaries/clarke/john/3.htm.
127. See John 3:30.
128. See Matthew 9:15, Mark 2:19-20, Luke 5:34-35.
129. Peter S. Williamson writes, "In both the Jewish and Greek cultures of that time, the immediate cosmetic preparation of the bride included a bath with fragrant oils so that she could be as clean and beautiful as possible. Baptism…is the Church's bridal bath that prepares her to be united with her bridegroom." Williamson, Peter. "Wives and Husbands, Christ and the Church." In *Ephesians (Catholic Commentary on Sacred Scripture)*, 166. Michigan, MI: Baker Academic, 2009.
130. See 2 Kings 17.
131. See Clarke's Commentary on 2 Kings 17:24. http://biblehub.com/commentaries/clarke/2_kings/17.htm.
132. See Life for Today Study Bible Notes on John 4:4.
133. See "Samaritan Pentateuch: in Easton's Bible Dictionary. https://www.blueletterbible.org/search/Dictionary/viewTopic.cfm?topic=ET0003203.
134. See Life for Today Study Bible Notes on John 4:4.
135. Bidmead, Julye. "Women and Wells in the Hebrew Bible." Bible Odyssey. http://www.bibleodyssey.org/places/related-articles/women-and-wells-in-the-hebrew-bible.aspx.
136. Pitre, Brant. "The Divine Love Story." In *Jesus the Bridegroom: The Greatest Love Story Ever Told*, 59. Kindle ed. Random House, 2014.
137. See Genesis 29.
138. See Clarke's Commentary on John 4:10. http://biblehub.com/commentaries/clarke/john/4.htm.
139. Pitre, Brant. "The Divine Love Story." In *Jesus the Bridegroom: The Greatest Love Story Ever Told*, 70. Kindle ed. Random House, 2014.
140. Typically the Mohar (bride price) was negotiated between the two fathers of the prospective couple. See Greenstone, Julius H., Joseph Jacobs, J. F. McLaughlin, Solomon Schechter, and Isidore Singer. "Marriage." Jewish Encyclopedia. http://www.jewishencyclopedia.com/articles/10432-marriage.
141. See Genesis 24:22 and 24:53.
142. McWhirter, Jocelyn. "The Johannine Jesus at Jacob's Well." In *The Bridegroom Messiah and the People of God: Marriage in the Fourth Gospel*, 65. Kindle ed. Cambridge University Press, 2006.
143. Pitre, Brant. "The Divine Love Story." In *Jesus the Bridegroom: The Greatest Love Story Ever Told*, 64. Kindle ed. Random House, 2014.
144. Sexuality and Christian Hope. Tim Keller. August 10, 2015. https://www.youtube.com/watch?v=WaYKyRLjxzI&list=PL_t3f7GgnX4hmEt-4ZOW0IMcwahIDA00eV.
145. "Samaria." Encyclopedia Britannica. https://www.britannica.com/place/Samaria-historical-region-Palestine.

Chapter 10: The Bride Price

146. See Benson Commentary on Zechariah 9:9. http://biblehub.com/commentaries/zechariah/9-9.htm.
147. See Exodus 12.
148. "Holidays and Festivals." Chosen People Ministries. http://www.chosenpeople.com/main/holidays-and-festivals/190-the-meaning-of-passover.
149. Also see Leviticus 3:17 and 7:26-27.
150. See John 6:35-67.
151. During the Passover meal there is a tradition to drink four cups of wine. The cup which Jesus refers to as the "cup of the new covenant" was the third cup in the meal known as the cup of redemption or blessing. http://www.jewsforjesus.org/files/pdf/newsletter/newsletter-2002-03.pdf
152. Amaral, Joe. "A Feast in Jerusalem." In *Understanding Jesus: Cultural Insights into the Words and Deeds of Christ*, 92-100. Milton, ON: Almond Publications, 2009.
153. True Easter Story - The Promise Kept. Directed by Ray VanderLaan. Zondervan, 2002. DVD.
154. Amaral, Joe. "A Feast in Jerusalem." In *Understanding Jesus: Cultural Insights into the Words and Deeds of Christ*, 93-95. Milton, ON: Almond Publications, 2009.
155. See Luke 22:44.
156. Amaral, Joe. "A Feast in Jerusalem." In *Understanding Jesus: Cultural Insights into the Words and Deeds of Christ*, 164-165. Milton, ON: Almond Publications, 2009.
157. Galatians 3:13 says, "But Christ has rescued us from the curse pronounced by the law. When he was hung on the cross, he took upon himself the curse for our wrongdoing. For it is written in the Scriptures, "Cursed is everyone who is hung on a tree.""
158. English Standard Version.
159. One of the cruelties of crucifixion was that the condemned would have to constantly push their body up on the cross in order to breathe. As his strength diminished, Jesus would have struggled to take in air causing a buildup of carbonic acid in his blood which would eventually lead to an irregular heartbeat. Since Jesus was already experiencing a great loss of blood, his increased heart rate would have also contributed to heart failure and allowed fluid to collect around his heart and lungs. When the soldier pierced his side, it is likely the spear entered his lung and punctured his heart which would have resulted in the gush of water and blood.
160. If you are interested in the historical evidence for the resurrection, I highly recommend Lee Strobel's book *The Case for Christ.*
161. English Standard Version.
162. See 1 John 4:13 and 1 Corinthians 3:16.
163. The Church is simply the name given for Christian believers.

Chapter 11: The Unveiling

164. See *Superman: The Wedding Album.*
165. English Standard Version.
166. Walker, Derek. "Mount Moriah and Golgotha." July 13, 2013. https://www.youtube.com/watch?v=X14Oh1ncvq8.
167. See Clarke's Commentary on Genesis 22:2. http://biblehub.com/commentaries/clarke/genesis/22.htm.
168. English Standard Version.
169. See Genesis 24:14.
170. Why did Rebekah freely offer herself to Abraham's servant in such a sacrificial way? I think there may be a spiritual truth we uncover in verse 15. "Before he had finished praying, he saw a young woman named Rebekah coming out with her water jug on her shoulder. She was the daughter of Bethuel, who was the son of Abraham's brother Nahor and his wife, Milcah." (Genesis 24:15). Rebekah was coming from her father's house. Her father's name was Bethuel, which means "house of God." Rebekah had spent her life dwelling in the house of God. Jesus desires a bride that dwells in God's presence. When one spends time in God's presence, they cannot help becoming more like him.
171. Genesis 24:67 says, "And Isaac brought Rebekah into his mother Sarah's tent, and she became his wife. He loved her deeply, and she was a special comfort to him after the death of his mother." This is the second time in the Bible the word "love" is used. Love was first mentioned to describe Abraham's love for Isaac. Here it is used a second time to describe Isaac's love for bride. We see a picture of the Father's perfect love being imparted to the Son who in turn imparts it to his bride.
172. See Genesis 25:11.
173. In the book of Revelation, John receives a vision of the future where he learns that Jesus will lead his Church to "springs of living water" which is similar to how Isaac leads Rebekah to the water of "the Living One." "For the Lamb in the midst of the throne will be their shepherd, and he will guide them to springs of living water, and God will wipe away every tear from their eyes." (Revelation 7:17 English Standard Version).
174. Valkanet, Rich. "Bible Timeline." 2010. http://biblehub.com/timeline.
175. 1 Corinthians 15:45.
176. See Genesis 2:21-2:22.
177. In John 15:13 Jesus says, "There is no greater love than to lay down one's life for one's friends."
178. See Strong's Concordance: "Apokalupsis." Bible Hub. http://biblehub.com/greek/602.htm.
179. New International Version.
180. English Standard Version.
181. See Revelation 22:8-9.
182. Genesis 2:23.
183. The ending of Revelation seems to echo the final verse in Song of Songs, which the Jews consider to be a love song between God and Israel.

"Come away, my love! Be like a gazelle or a young stag on the mountains of spices." (Song of Songs 8:14).

Chapter 12: Boy + Girl = Divine Plan

184. Sharkey, Linda. "Average British Woman Spends £140,000 on Hair and Cosmetics in Her Lifetime, Research Reveals." September 14, 2014. http://www.independent.co.uk/life-style/fashion/news/the-staggering-average-lifetime-spend-on-cosmetics-and-grooming-revealed-9709654.html.
185. De Lacy, Martha. "Women Spend More Time Checking out OTHER WOMEN than They Do Men (and It's Their Clothes, Figures and Hair We're Most Interested In)." 2012. http://www.dailymail.co.uk/femail/article-2232842/Women-spend-time-checking-OTHER-WOMEN-men-clothes-figures-hair-interested-in.html.
186. New International Version.
187. 1 Samuel 13:14.
188. Hale, Mandy. "What (Most) Women Really Want." The Single Woman. February 2, 2016. http://thesinglewoman.net/2016/02/02/what-most-women-really-want.
189. "Six Things Women Wish They Could Tell Men." Eharmony.com. http://www.eharmony.com/dating-advice/relationships/six-things-women-wish-they-could-tell-men/#.VuDWEpwrKUk.
190. Women also reveal God's gentle, nurturing spirit. God is sometimes portrayed as an angry old man that wants to zap sinners from the sky and this description completely misses the mark. Isaiah 66:13 says, "As a mother comforts her child, so will I comfort you…" (NIV). God's gentle and forgiving nature is revealed in women.
191. English Standard Version.
192. See Galatians 5:16-25.
193. See Ephesians 5:21-29.
194. Velthouse, Lisa. "Hot and Holy." October 1, 2013. http://www.christianitytoday.com/ct/2013/october/meaning-of-sex-hot-and-holy.html.
195. For more details I recommend the books *The Case for Marriage* by Linda Waite and Maggie Gallagher and *Hooked: New Science on how Casual Sex is Affecting our Children* by Joe Mcllhaney Jr and Freda Mckissic Bush.
196. Stanton, Glenn. "How We Dishonor God in Our Sex Lives." Focus on the Family. 2004. Accessed October 1, 2015. http://www.focusonthefamily.com/marriage/sex-and-intimacy/gods-design-for-sex/how-we-dishonor-god-in-our-sex-lives.
197. Keller, Timothy, and Kathy Keller. "Sex and Marriage." In *The Meaning of Marriage: Facing the Complexities of Commitment with the Wisdom of God*, 260. New York, NY: Dutton, 2011.
198. Keller, Timothy, and Kathy Keller. "The Essence of Marriage." In *The Meaning of Marriage: Facing the Complexities of Commitment with the Wisdom*

of God, 80. New York, NY: Dutton, 2011.

199. Jackson, Rob. "The Sexual-Spiritual Union of a Man and Woman." Focus on the Family. 2004. http://www.focusonthefamily.com/marriage/sex-and-intimacy/gods-design-for-sex/sexual-spiritual-union.
200. Piper, John. "Sex and the Supremacy of Christ, Part 1." September 24, 2004. http://www.desiringgod.org/messages/sex-and-the-supremacy-of-christ-part-1.
201. Kreeft, Peter. "The Fiercest Battle." In *How to Win the Culture War: A Christian Battle Plan for a Society in Crisis*, 95. Downers Grove, IL: InterVarsity Press, 2002.
202. Keller, Timothy, and Kathy Keller. "Sex and Marriage." In *The Meaning of Marriage: Facing the Complexities of Commitment with the Wisdom of God*, 271. New York, NY: Dutton, 2011.
203. Piper, John. "Forgiving and Forbearing." In *This Momentary Marriage: A Parable of Permanence*. Kindle ed. Wheaton, IL: Crossway Books, 2009.
204. Alcorn, Randy. "Sex in Heaven?" June 12, 2014. http://www.desiringgod.org/interviews/sex-in-heaven.
205. West, Christopher. "Conjugal Life and Liturgical Life." In *Heaven's Song: Sexual Love as It Was Meant to Be*. Kindle ed. West Chester, PA: Ascension Press, 2008.

Chapter 13: Love Story

206. Keller, Timothy, and Kathy Keller. "Sex and Marriage." In *The Meaning of Marriage: Facing the Complexities of Commitment with the Wisdom of God*, 179. New York, NY: Dutton, 2011.

207. It is important to remember that submission is a divine role in the Trinity. Jesus willingly submits to the Father with joy. When the Bible calls wives to submit to their husbands, our culture is appalled; but the Bible also calls husbands to love their wives as Christ loved the Church. The Bible does not teach that a wife must submit to a husband in everything. If a husband calls her to do anything that violates scripture she is obligated to disobey.

    Contrary to restricting women, some of the most radically pro-women ideas in history come from the Bible. Ephesians 5:24-28 says, "As the church submits to Christ, so you wives should submit to your husbands in everything. [25] For husbands, this means love your wives, just as Christ loved the church. He gave up his life for her [26] to make her holy and clean, washed by the cleansing of God's word. [27] He did this to present her to himself as a glorious church without a spot or wrinkle or any other blemish. Instead, she will be holy and without fault. [28] In the same way, husbands ought to love their wives as they love their own bodies. For a man who loves his wife actually shows love for himself." In the 1st century when this was written, wives were considered the property of their husbands and their primary duty was to serve and produce children. That a husband was called to love his wife as an equal would have been considered absurd. 1

Corinthians 7:3-4 says, "The husband should fulfill his wife's sexual needs, and the wife should fulfill her husband's needs. The wife gives authority over her body to her husband, and the husband gives authority over his body to his wife." This teaching was completely radical in the patriarchal society of the day. Just because something in the Bible is countercultural does not mean it should be thrown out. If that was the case, it would have been justified for men to take advantage of their wives in ancient times because it was part of the culture.

208. New International Version.
209. Sheets, Dutch. "The Dance." In *Pleasure of His Company, The: A Journey to Intimate Friendship With God*. Kindle ed. Bloomington, MN: Bethany House, 2014.
210. New International Version.
211. Quest." Merriam-Webster. http://www.merriam-webster.com/dictionary/quest.

Chapter 14: Flashback to Eternity

212. See Deuteronomy 30:6.
213. Macpherson, Alex. "Taylor Swift: 'I Want to Believe in Pretty Lies'" The Guardian, 18 Oct. 2012. Web. http://www.theguardian.com/music/2012/oct/18/taylor-swift-want-believe-pretty-lies.
214. Klein, John, and Adam Spears. Lost in Translation Vol. 1: Rediscovering the Hebrew Roots of Our Faith. Kindle ed. 2007.
215. Piper, John. "Multnomah." In *Desiring God*, 18. Multnomah, 2003.

Made in the USA
Columbia, SC
26 April 2017